One of John Hughes's most charmingly offbeat films, **Ferris Bueller's Day Off** is certainly among the most overtly humorous of his canon of teen movies. It is also one of his best-remembered, its profile challenged only by the acclaimed *The Breakfast Club* which was released the year beforehand. Contrasting perfectly with the more serious, issue-based tone of *Pretty in Pink* which immediately preceded it in the same year, Hughes's wittily incisive dialogue was never as razor-sharp as when delivered by the smart-mouthed high school slacker Ferris Bueller.

MEDIA, FEMINISM, CULTURAL STUDIES

The Poetry of Cinema
by John Madden

The Sacred Cinema of Andrei Tarkovsky
by Jeremy Mark Robinson

Jean-Luc Godard: The Passion of Cinema / Le Passion de Cinéma
by Jeremy Mark Robinson

Liv Tyler
by Thomas A. Christie

Disney Business, Disney Films, Disney Lands
The Wonderful World of the Walt Disney Company
Daniel Cerruti

Steven Spielberg: God-light
by Jeremy Mark Robinson

Francis Coppola
by Jeremy Mark Robinson

Stepping Forward: Essays, Lectures and Interviews
by Wolfgang Iser

Wild Zones: Pornography, Art and Feminism
by Kelly Ives

'Cosmo Woman': The World of Women's Magazines
by Oliver Whitehorne

Paul Verhoeven
by Jeremy Mark Robinson

George Lucas
by Jeremy Mark Robinson

Stanley Kubrick
by Jeremy Mark Robinson

Walerian Borowczyk
by Jeremy Mark Robinson

Andrea Dworkin
by Jeremy Mark Robinson

Cixous, Irigaray, Kristeva: The Jouissance of French Feminism
by Kelly Ives

Sex in Art: Pornography and Pleasure in Painting and Sculpture
by Cassidy Hughes

*The Erotic Object: Sexuality in Sculpture
From Prehistory to the Present Day*
by Susan Quinnell

Women in Pop Music
by Helen Challis

Detonation Britain: Nuclear War in the UK
by Jeremy Mark Robinson

Julia Kristeva: Art, Love, Melancholy, Philosophy, Semiotics
by Kelly Ives

Luce Irigaray: Lips, Kissing, and the Politics of Sexual Difference
by Kelly Ives

Helene Cixous I Love You: The Jouissance of Writing
by Kelly Ives

Feminism and Shakespeare
by B.D. Barnacle

About the Author

Thomas Christie has a life-long fascination with films and the people who make them. Currently reading for a PhD in Scottish Literature, he lives in Scotland with his family.

He holds a first-class Honours degree in Literature and a Masters degree in Humanities, specialising with distinction in British Cinema History, from the Open University in Milton Keynes, England.

He is the author of *Liv Tyler, Star in Ascendance: Her First Decade in Film* (2007), *The Cinema of Richard Linklater* (2008), and a book on John Hughes' 1980s cinema (2010), which are also published by Crescent Moon.

**Ferris Bueller's Day Off
Pocket Movie Guide**

Ferris Bueller's Day Off

Pocket Movie Guide

Thomas A. Christie

Crescent Moon

Crescent Moon Publishing
P.O. Box 393
Maidstone
Kent
ME14 5XU, U.K.

First edition 2011.
© Thomas A. Christie 2011.

Printed and bound in the U.S.A.
Set in Helvetica Neue Condensed.
Designed by Radiance Graphics.

The right of Thomas A. Christie to be identified as the author of this book has been asserted generally in accordance with sections 77 and 78 of the Copyright, Designs and Patents Act 1988.

All rights reserved. No part of this book may be reprinted or reproduced, stored in a retrieval system, or transmitted, in any form or by any means, electronic, mechanical, photocopying, recording or otherwise, without permission from the publisher.

British Library Cataloguing in Publication data available for this title.

Christie, Thomas A.
Ferris Bueller's Day Off: Pocket Movie Guide
I. Title
791.4'33

ISBN-13 9781861713063

COPYRIGHT NOTICE

This text includes references to organisations, feature films, television programmes, popular songs, musical bands, novels and reference books, the titles of which are Trademarks and/or Registered Trademarks, and which are the intellectual properties of their respective copyright holders.

PICTURE CREDITS

Every effort has been made to contact copyright owners of the illustrations. No copyright infringement is intended. We welcome enquiries about any copyright issues for future editions of this book.

CONTENTS

Illustrations 9

1 The Movie 11
2 The Cast 25
3 The Locations 40
4 The Music 45
5 Scene-by-Scene Analysis 52

Filmography 97
Theatrical Release Dates 99
Release Information 100
The Films of John Hughes: A Timeline 102
Further Reading 106
Illustrations 108

MATTHEW BRODERICK

BUELLER... BUELLER... EDITION

1

FERRIS BUELLER'S DAY OFF

THE MOVIE

One of John Hughes's (1950-2009) most charmingly offbeat films, *Ferris Bueller's Day Off* (1986) is certainly among the most overtly humorous of his canon of teen movies. It is also one of his best-remembered, its profile challenged only by the acclaimed *The Breakfast Club* which was released the year beforehand. Contrasting perfectly with the more serious, issue-based tone of *Pretty in Pink* which immediately preceded it in the same year,[1] Hughes's wittily incisive dialogue was never as razor-sharp as when delivered by the smart-mouthed high school slacker Ferris Bueller. Cool as ice, massively popular with everyone he meets and seemingly impossible to outsmart, Ferris was the teenager with all the answers; the kind of person who everyone growing up in an eighties high school wanted to be.

The film came about during a particularly fertile period in John Hughes's filmography. By the time of its release, Hughes had developed a very successful career – in a remarkably short period of time – both as a screenwriter and later as a director. He had provided the scripts for comedies such as Michael Miller's *National Lampoon's Class Reunion* (1982), Stan Dragoti's *Mr Mom* (1983) and Harold Ramis's celebrated *National Lampoon's*

Vacation (1983) before making an impressive directorial debut with *Sixteen Candles* (1984), the film which was to mark the beginning of his now-legendary cycle of teen movies. Throughout the course of the mid-eighties, Hughes would reshape all expectations of what the genre could offer, exploring deep emotional and socio-cultural issues in ways that were relevant not just to teenagers, but to audiences of all ages. He managed, with a success that his contemporaries were seldom to match, to provide a wry but always contemplative standpoint on topics that were significant to the teen audiences of the time, delving into their fears and desires in ways that never trivialised or patronised them. Whether in the profound deliberations of *The Breakfast Club* (1985) or the fantastical whimsy of *Weird Science* (1985), Hughes always achieved a lightness of touch in his approach to his subject matter, effortlessly combining the absurd and the commonplace to create an interesting, skilfully-crafted take on life, replete with all of its authentic disorderliness and random illogicalities.

As the penultimate film in Hughes's cycle of six teen movies in the eighties, *Ferris Bueller's Day Off* is an interestingly pitched feature. Filmed between 9 September and 22 November 1985,[2] it is considerably more light-hearted in tone than the socially-conscious class anxieties of *Pretty in Pink* (1986) which was released before it in the same year, and yet with its sense of wistful, understated remorse at the passing of fleeting youth the film also foreshadows the uncertainty and sporadic emotional melancholy which are evident throughout in *Some Kind of Wonderful* (1987), Hughes's final teen film of the decade. Hughes not only occupied the director's chair for the filming of *Ferris Bueller's Day Off*, but was also to assume production and scriptwriting responsibilities. Cast in the title role was the talented Matthew Broderick, who had been enjoying critical and commercial success at the time thanks to his performances in features including John Badham's *WarGames* (1983), Herbert Ross's *Max Dugan Returns* (1983), and Richard Donner's *Ladyhawke* (1985). His unforgettable appearance as Hughes's eponymous hero was to ensure that Ferris Bueller would become one of Broderick's best-known performances, and indeed it remains one of his most fondly-remembered amongst audiences even today.

Ferris Bueller's Day Off went on general release in America on 11 June 1986. The only other film making its debut in the United States that day was Gabriel Auer's drama *Les Yeux des Oiseaux* (*The Eyes of the Birds*), starring Roland Amstutz and Carlos Andreu, following its initial 1983 release in France. Hughes's film did very well at the box-office, accruing a domestic gross of $70,136,369,[3] having been filmed on an estimated budget of only $6,000,000.[4] (Indeed, the film was so immediately successful with audiences that it had made its money back in full during the opening weekend – $6,275,647 was the figure put on the box-office takings as of 15 June 1986.)[5] As a result, *Ferris Bueller's Day Off* became one of the year's biggest hits in American cinemas, charting in the top ten of the highest grossing films in the United States that year (the biggest box-office smash of 1986 being Tony Scott's military action drama *Top Gun*, closely followed by Peter Faiman's celebrated fish-out-of-water comedy *Crocodile Dundee*). This is particularly noteworthy given the strong competition in cinemas throughout the same year of release. 1986 was something of a vintage year for eighties American cinema, with many noteworthy releases from prominent directors which included David Lynch's *Blue Velvet*, James Cameron's *Aliens*, Rob Reiner's *Stand By Me*, Woody Allen's *Hannah and Her Sisters*, Oliver Stone's *Salvador*, David Cronenberg's *The Fly*, and Roland Joffe's *The Mission*, to name but a few. The Academy Awards for that year's cinematic output also reflected the wide variety of dramatic quality on offer, celebrating films such as Martin Scorsese's *The Color of Money* (Paul Newman as Best Actor) and Randa Haines's *Children of a Lesser God* (Marlee Matlin as Best Actress), while the Best Director Award went to Oliver Stone for his powerful Vietnam War drama *Platoon*, which was also awarded Best Picture (as well as receiving numerous other nominations at the same ceremony).

Ferris Bueller's Day Off is a film of many deftly-employed contradictions. It is a movie about high school students which only rarely features high school, and features a dense narrative that celebrates the family whilst also emphasising the harm that can be caused by domestic tensions. Yet following the comparatively staid approach of *Pretty in Pink*, Hughes never allows issue-based drama to subordinate the film's humour, leaving the audience in no doubt that *Ferris Bueller's Day Off* signalled a return to comedy both sophisticated and farcical. From Ferris's urbane wisecracks to the outrageous pratfalls suffered by his high school's dean Ed Rooney (Jeffrey Jones), the film employs a wide variety of comedic approaches with a high degree of success throughout.

The film also features, in Ferris, one of Hughes's most distinctive protagonists; the character passed almost instantly into the annals of modern film history, becoming one of the best-loved popular cultural icons of the 1980s. Ferris was fun-loving and affluent, but also smart and appealing. Although he could be self-centred at times, he was also sympathetic, generous with his time and his advice. And although the film sees him revelling in his youth, determined to make the most of his receding teen years before the inevitable passage into adulthood, the larger-than-life Ferris is possessed of a thoughtful enough personality to realise that life is only ever what an individual makes of it. Much of the film centres on his resolve to write his own rules for both his present and future, rather than being forced to slavishly obey those which are imposed upon his peers by aloof authority figures. Ferris is the living embodiment of William Blake's famous assertion that one must adopt his or her own unique and personal approach to life, lest they face the inescapable alternative of being confined by someone else's philosophies and principles instead.

Matthew Broderick delivers a superb performance as Ferris, and indeed his handling of this charming, imperturbable protagonist is vastly to his credit. Given the character's deviously manipulative nature and sometimes vaguely conceited manner, it may seem easy – at face value – for the viewer to quickly develop contempt for Ferris. But in the hands of Broderick and Hughes he instead becomes a kind of champion for eighties youth, his lifeaffirming attitudes and infectious sense of mischief making him almost impossible to dislike. Ferris's dexterous ability to out-manoeuvre his parents – and, by extension, the authorities in general – has made him a hero amongst his peers in the film, while news of his ersatz illnesses has been so convincingly propagated around the community that everyone from his school teachers to the emergency services are rooting for his recovery. (A running joke features endless floral arrangements being delivered to the Bueller family home from well-wishers, and non-stop local media coverage of Ferris's 'plight'.) Yet for all of his slacker genius and graceful sleight of hand in dealing with the adult world, the character is not without his deeper side.[6] Hughes uses admirable restraint in sketching out Ferris's concern for his uptight best friend Cameron (Alan Ruck), whom he worries is in danger of sleepwalking into a miserable adulthood due to his discontented upbringing by aloof, dysfunctional parents. (Ruck's performance as the anxious Cameron is all the more remarkable given that, far from being a teenager himself, the fresh-faced actor was actually in his late twenties at the time of filming.) Hughes is equally understated in his exploration of Ferris's affection for his beautiful and astute girlfriend Sloane (Mia Sara). The dichotomy between the characters' shared fondness for each other, and the knowledge that college and adult life may well force them to drift apart, is delineated with considerable care, and is always well-played by both Broderick and Sara.

Another reason for the success of *Ferris Bueller's Day Off* is its exceptional supporting cast; there is no weak link in a flawless roll-call of performers, all of whom bring something of value to the film. Most prominent among them is Jeffrey Jones, who steals every scene he appears in as the self-important, authoritarian dean of students Ed Rooney. Surely a spiritual cousin of *The Breakfast Club*'s similarly dictatorial Principal Vernon, Rooney is one of the film's standout characters, and Jones delivers a performance of comic genius in his depiction of the increasingly unhinged dean. As Ferris outwits the boggling grotesque at every turn, Rooney grows ever more desperate in his attempts to expose his scheming and bunking off – a path which eventually leads Rooney to unabashed criminality such as stalking and housebreaking, with some major animal cruelty along the way. Active in television and film since the early 1970s, at the time of *Ferris Bueller's Day Off* Jones was perhaps best-known for his Golden Globe-nominated performance as Emperor Joseph II in

Milos Forman's *Amadeus* (1984), and he brings all of his considerable comedic talents to bear on the slow disintegration of Rooney's dignity (and, quite possibly, the character's sanity). From his frustrated interactions with his hopeless secretary Grace (a brilliantly pitched turn by Edie McClurg) to his magnificently tongue-tied telephone conversation with Sloane's grieving but assertive father (actually Cameron, disguising his voice), Jones's superb comic performance ensured that Rooney was to become one of the most memorable of all of John Hughes's characters. He even makes the end credits sequence worth watching, as the pained reactions of the bruised and humiliated dean – forced to hitch a ride on the school bus – prove to be absolutely priceless.

Ferris's hard-working but ultimately rather gullible parents are both well portrayed by Lyman Ward and Cindy Pickett, who effectively combine their concern for their 'gravely ill' son with an assiduous dedication to their respective jobs, making them among the most sympathetically rendered parents to feature in any of Hughes's teen movies. But the trademark Hughesian portrait of distant adults who have difficulty relating to modern youth is still expertly articulated in the film thanks to Jonathan Schmock's marvellously condescending maitre d' of the upmarket Chez Quis restaurant, and most especially Ben Stein's monotonously droning economics teacher, whose teaching style is so dull that it verges on the hypnotic, reminding us of just why Ferris is so desperate to skip school in the first place.

Like many of Hughes's other teen films, a majority of the adult characters are often presented somewhat less magnanimously than those of the more youthful members of the cast. As noted, this is particularly obvious in the case of Ed Rooney, whose single-minded obsession with catching Ferris red-handed in the act of truancy stems from a wider anxiety at the erosion of his own authority within the school. Ferris's constant ability to outsmart Rooney throughout high school has been a persistent source of irritation to the older man, unconsciously making him resent his own complete lack of ability to predict Ferris's next move. This specifically antipathetic motivation is absent from other members of staff, such as Ben Stein's economics teacher or Del Close's literature teacher, who seem quite content to simply muddle on with their jobs – even though the students in their respective classes are uninterested in responding to their interminably dull questioning, not least due to the coma-inducing dullness of their delivery. Yet Hughes is also at pains to emphasise that although some educators like Rooney may be interpreted as the film's adversaries (that is, as archetypal establishment figures), education itself is most definitely never portrayed as the enemy. Ferris and his friends are intelligent, savvy, independently-minded and ambitious... even if their long-term aspirations sometimes appear unfocused. They have firm intentions to attend further education after leaving school, but their uncompromising individual autonomy suggests that their academic achievements have been accomplished in spite of a terminally jaded education system rather than because of it. And this, perhaps, is the crux of Rooney's loathing towards Ferris: in the teenager's seemingly-effortless ability to evade authoritarian convention and forge his own path, he is actively succeeding exactly where Rooney has failed in his own life. As had been the case with Paul Gleason's Richard Vernon the previous year, Rooney – an antagonistic exponent of the education system – has ultimately lost sight of the promise of his own youth, begrudging the freethinking mavericks in his charge for their gleeful nonconformity while hopelessly attempting to shore up a fatigued façade of authority that has earned the respect of no-one, including his own peers.

Yet for all the thought-provoking focus on the motivations of the adult characters, the film works even more effectively when it focuses on its young cast of actors, and Broderick is ably supported by Alan Ruck and Mia Sara as Ferris's two partners in crime. Ruck, who had appeared in a variety of prominent youth features in the early eighties including Lewis John Carlino's *Class* (1983) and Rick Rosenthal's *Bad Boys* (1983), puts in an admirably multifaceted performance as the twitchily neurotic Cameron, who finds himself overcoming long-held phobias as the day progresses until he is forced to confront his demons – and, indeed, his father. Although exploring the theme of familial friction in an otherwise lighthearted film may, in lesser hands, have seemed overwrought and awkward, Hughes makes Cameron's emotional journey a believable and touching one which fits perfectly into the narrative of the film. Indeed, Cameron's voyage from melancholy into psychological enlightenment contrasts very skilfully with Rooney's concurrent descent from despotic primacy into humiliation and eventual oblivion. Mia Sara, best-known at the time for her appearance in Ridley Scott's *Legend* (1985), is also very effective in the role of Ferris's knowing and resourceful girlfriend Sloane. The character seems full of admiration for Ferris's underlying good nature, even when he is cheerfully rewriting everyone's rulebook, and Sara's onscreen chemistry with Broderick is never less than convincing throughout. Jennifer Grey also impresses as Ferris's resentful sister Jeanie, who begrudges her brother's endless scheming for his own benefit while she, conversely, seems incapable of getting away with anything. Grey had appeared in a variety of films by the mid-eighties including John Milius's *Red Dawn* (1984) and Francis Ford Coppola's *The Cotton Club* (1984), and would later go on to huge success in one of the eighties' most memorable box-office hits – Emile Ardolino's *Dirty Dancing* (1987) – where her performance as Frances 'Baby' Houseman was to earn her a nomination for a Golden Globe award.

Ferris Bueller's Day Off was one of Hughes's most accomplished and fully-rounded works as director, and his skilful location shooting makes the most of everything that Illinois has to offer. The film has sometimes been called his love letter to Chicago, and it would be difficult to deny that his obvious affection for the city's atmosphere and inhabitants shines through from almost every frame. From striking shots of the Windy City's famously iconic skyscrapers to a whistle-stop travelogue of its landmarks and vibrant cultural identity, and from the leafy Illinois suburbs to the dismal corridors of Ocean Park High School, the film is never less than a constant treat of visual variety. Jennifer Polito's excellent set design is also worthy of mention – especially in the case of Ferris's typically idiosyncratic room, a veritable masterpiece of top-flight teen paraphernalia and cutting edge eighties accoutrements. The film marked an interesting side-step for Hughes with its appealing device of having Ferris addressing the audience directly, breaking the fourth wall with much aplomb as his offbeat protagonist frankly discusses his thoughts on the action throughout the course of the film. The action is accompanied by a rousing score provided by industry veteran Ira Newborn, perhaps best known for his work on the *Police Squad!* (1982) television series, and its cinematic spin-off, David Zucker's *The Naked Gun* (1988). Someone who had worked with Hughes on a number of occasions – he had earlier provided the soundtrack for *Weird Science* in 1985, and would later score *Planes, Trains and Automobiles* in 1987 and *Uncle Buck* in 1989 – Newborn has also composed music for films as diverse as Tom Mankiewicz's *Dragnet* (1987), Tom Shadyac's *Ace Ventura: Pet Detective* (1994) and Kevin Smith's *Mallrats* (1995).

With all of its light-heartedness and *joie-de-vivre*, *Ferris Bueller's Day Off* has remained a popular fixture of the teen movie genre even a quarter of a century after its first release in American cinemas. Like *The Breakfast Club*, the universality of the themes presented by Hughes allow the film's key issues – encouraging freedom from stifling conformity, and upholding the autonomy of free will beyond the confines of mainstream expectation – to transcend the now-dated fashions and styles of the eighties. Indeed, it is also a film which celebrates culture in all of its forms, for at times Hughes embraces not only American culture, but also that of many different eras and nationalities. From the director's subtle references to Beatles songs scattered throughout the film's dialogue to the stately showcasing of the treasure trove of artwork on display at the Art Institute of Chicago (Picasso, Rodin, Modigliani and Pollock among them), *Ferris Bueller's Day Off* pays homage to many different artistic influences which have come to impact upon modern culture. Yet in turn, the film has also helped to indelibly influence popular culture from the time of its production onwards. A great many of its elements have been referenced, parodied and imitated over the years in TV series and other films, from the desirability and demolition of Mr Frye's immaculate Ferrari to the economics teacher's monotonic class roll-call, and from Ferris's witty but thoughtful asides to camera through to Cameron's rousing speech as he prepares to stand up to his tyrannical father for the first time in his life. Nor, for the many people who have seen the film, has it ever been possible to view some of Chicago's landmarks in quite the same way again – to say nothing of the city's Von Steuben Day parade. It is no exaggeration to say that *Ferris Bueller's Day Off* is among the most influential of all eighties films, and one of the single most culturally significant of the entire teen movie genre.

Yet for all its universal themes and enduring appeal, the film is also undeniably a product of its time. Released against a backdrop of Cold War tensions and Western capitalistic excess, Hughes's movie exhibits an interesting take on the issues of the mid-eighties, most especially Reaganomics. The main characters are all white, middle-class and affluent, which suggests a rather restricted view of social issues within the film, and yet it always feels obvious that Hughes is so focused on presenting topics of common relevance that the class and demographic origin of the characters is more or less a secondary consideration. The venues sampled by Ferris and his friends in Chicago are an interesting blend of the free or inexpensive (the Sears Tower observation deck and the visitors' centre at the Chicago Board of Trade) and the upmarket and costly (the exclusive Chez Quis restaurant, or choice seats at Wrigley Field), suggesting that what matters is the quality and range of the experiences at hand rather than the ostentation implied by their financial cost. It is also obvious from Ferris's home and cutting-edge (for the time) technological accoutrements that his family is at least comfortably off; Cameron's household – complete with vintage car collection – is quite probably even more so. Yet while money is clearly not a limiting factor for Ferris, quite in contrast to the key themes of *Pretty in Pink* and *Some Kind of Wonderful*, Hughes seemed more inclined to explore the goals that lie outwith the reach of capital gain. Ferris's love for Sloane and fraternal affection for Cameron, for instance, are both factors that are at risk from the encroaching but inevitable advance of adulthood; nor can any amount of hard cash fully dispel the attempts of the establishment to force Ferris (and, more specifically, his generation at large) to fit into a conveniently manageable pigeonhole – an endeavour which he is hell-bent on opposing at all costs. Thus while prosperity and wealth are one means of liberation that the film examines, albeit in a fairly low-key manner, Hughes appears keen to emphasise that an individual's quality of life is actually composed of a complicated patchwork of needs and desires, many of which that will always be unobtainable by pecuniary means.

Ferris Bueller's Day Off proved to be one of the most critically successful of all Hughes's films, with commentators of the time praising it for its easy-going charm,[7] the engaging charisma of its central character,[8] and aptitude for skilfully implemented comedy situations.[9] The few dissenting critical voices were disparaging of what they perceived to be a jarring break from the realism of most (though certainly not all) of Hughes's earlier teen movies,[10] and – on the other hand – an alleged inability to take full advantage of the film's anarchic central premise.[11] However, negative criticism was largely in the minority, and the generally affirmative attitude towards *Ferris Bueller's Day Off* has continued into the present day. Recent appraisals of the film have been upbeat and constructive, with reviewers approving of its highly proficient pacing,[12] considerable hidden depths of characterisation,[13] and the fact that Ferris's affability and unshakeable slacker credentials have managed to stand the test of time.[14] The film's widespread critical success was to translate into other recognition: his starring role as Ferris Bueller was to see Matthew Broderick nominated for a Golden Globe award for Best Performance by an Actor in a Motion Picture (Comedy/Musical) in 1987. Indeed, it remains one of his most instantly recognisable roles of the eighties, even taking into account many other high-profile film performances later in the decade which included Jonathan Kaplan's *Project X* (1987), Mike Nichols's *Biloxi Blues* (1988) and Paul Bogart's *Torch Song Trilogy* (1988).

The film's popularity also led to the creation of a short-lived television series, *Ferris Bueller*, which was broadcast on NBC between 1990 and 1991. The series starred Charlie Schlatter as Ferris, and shifted the action from Illinois to California. Many of the film's main characters were to feature in the televised situation comedy, though all were played by different actors, and the events depicted in Hughes's film were not referenced directly in the series. In spite of an able ensemble cast which included Jennifer Aniston as Jeanie, Brandon Douglas as Cameron, Ami Dolenz as Sloane and Richard Riehle as Ed Rooney, the series lasted for only thirteen episodes before being cancelled, and – unlike the film which originated it – the TV series has become an obscure curiosity which is little-known today.

Interestingly, *Ferris Bueller's Day Off* has established itself not only as a favourite feature amongst fans of Hughes's oeuvre, but as a lasting fixture in American cinema. It has transcended the era of its production in a manner that has allowed it to remain relevant to audiences in ways that so few films ever have, either before or since. Even though it has naturally established itself as a key work of nostalgia for anyone who had been a teenager in the eighties, it has somehow developed into something much more than that. From its oft-repeated catchphrases to its distinctive imagery, Hughes succeeded in leaving an indelible imprint on the American cinema of the late twentieth century; an imprimatur that states, in the clearest and boldest possible terms, that individuality and personal liberty are values which cannot be compromised. This ongoing celebration of the film's invigorating celebration of self-determination has manifested itself in many ways, but perhaps none quite so distinctive as Project Bueller, an ambitious undertaking organised by artists Kara Suhey and Mina Karimi to re-enact the famous Von Steuben Day Parade scene – with the aid of carefully chosen look-alikes – transposing the action from Chicago's Dearborn Street to New York's famous Village Halloween Parade in 2008.[15]

Ferris Bueller's Day Off is one of Hughes's best-regarded teen movies, and it has also become one of the most critically and commercially successful comedies in his entire filmography. With enough wit and style to win over audiences of all ages, *Ferris Bueller's Day Off* tapped into the eighties zeitgeist so effectively that it quickly established itself as one of the most fondly-remembered film comedies of the decade amongst many commentators and Hughes fans alike. Indeed, the film's energy and nostalgic charm has led to its repeated re-release on video, DVD and Blu-Ray over the years since its original cinematic release. Its continued popularity with audiences even today proves that the themes of liberation and self-determination presented by Hughes remain as universal and as relevant in the twenty-first century as they had been back in the eighties.

References

1. The way in which *Ferris Bueller's Day Off* fits into Hughes's wider canon of films is discussed in the following text: Quentin J. Schultze, Roy M. Anker, James D. Bratt, William D. Romanowski, John W. Worst and Lambert Zuidervaart, *Dancing in the Dark: Youth, Popular Culture, and the Electronic Media* (Grand Rapids: William B. Eerdmans Publishing, 1990), pp.230-232.
2. Production data from *www.imdb.com*.
<http://www.imdb.com/title/tt0091042/business>
3. Box office data from *www.boxofficemojo.com*.
<http://www.boxofficemojo.com/movies/?id=ferrisbuellersdayoff.htm>
4. Budgetary data from *www.imdb.com*.
< http://www.imdb.com/title/tt0091042/business>
5. Box office data from *www.imdb.com*.
<http://www.imdb.com/title/tt0091042/business>
6. Janet Staiger presents a highly detailed theoretical analysis of Ferris Bueller (both the character and the film) in her valuable book *Perverse Spectators*: Janet Staiger, *Perverse Spectators: The Practices of Film Reception* (New York: New York University Press, 2000), pp.118-123.
7. Roger Ebert, '*Ferris Bueller's Day Off*', in *The Chicago Sun-Times*, 11 June 1986.
8. Rob Salem, 'Adults are the idiots in tale of two kiddies', in *The Toronto Star*, 13 June 1986.
9. Bob Thomas, 'At the Movies: *Ferris Bueller's Day Off*', in *The Associated Press*, 26 June 1986.
10. Nina Darnton, 'Screen: A Youth's *Day Off*', in *The New York Times*, 11 June 1986.
11. Patrick Goldstein, 'Director Has an Off Day in *Day Off*', in *The Los Angeles Times*, 20 June 1986.
12. Noel Megahey, '*Ferris Bueller's Day Off*: Bueller... Bueller... Edition', in *DVD Times*, 29 March 2006.
<http://www.dvdtimes.co.uk/content.php?contentid=60991>
13. Adam Smith, 'Empire Essay: *Ferris Bueller's Day Off*', in *Empire Online*, 5 May 2008.
<http://www.empireonline.com/reviews/reviewcomplete.asp?FID=132851>
14. Gary Panton, '*Ferris Bueller's Day Off*', in *Movie Gazette*, 9 July 2003.
<http://www.movie-gazette.com/cinereviews/313>
15. Amos Barshad, 'Project Bueller is Back!', in *New York*

Magazine, 1 October 2008.
   <http://nymag.com/daily/entertainment/2008/10/project_bueller_is_back.html>
   See also: <http://projectbueller.tumblr.com/>

2

FERRIS BUELLER'S DAY OFF

THE CAST

One of the reasons for the lasting success of Ferris Bueller's Day Off *can be found in its excellent ensemble cast. From the three compelling main leads to the actors behind Hughes's faultlessly selected constellation of dysfunctional adults, the film has long been revered for the strength of its performances – in all of their eccentric, frenzied and sometimes contemplative glory. This chapter examines the careers, before and after, of the artists who breathed life into the characters of* Ferris Bueller's Day Off.

MATTHEW BRODERICK (Ferris Bueller)

Matthew Broderick made his cinematic debut in the role of Michael McPhee in Herbert Ross's *Max Dugan Returns* (1983), a well-received drama which was written by Neil Simon. He also had prominent leading roles as computer whiz-kid David Lightman, who comes close to accidentally triggering World War III in John Badham's *WarGames* (1983), and as the cursed thief Philippe Gaston in Richard Donner's *Ladyhawke* (1985).

Additionally, he appeared in two historical dramas directed by Ken Harrison, *1918* (1985) and *On Valentine's Day* (1986).

Following the success of *Ferris Bueller's Day Off*, Broderick remained highly visible in the world of eighties cinema, starring in a diverse range of films which included Jonathan Kaplan's science fiction thriller *Project X* (1987), Mike Nichols's World War II military drama *Biloxi Blues* (1988) (which, like Broderick's acting debut, was based upon a Neil Simon screenplay), Paul Bogart's New York-based romantic comedy *Torch Song Trilogy* (1988), and Sidney Lumet's crime-based comedy-drama *Family Business* (1989), where he starred alongside Sean Connery and Dustin Hoffman. Perhaps most prominent of all was his performance as Colonel Robert Gould Shaw in Edward Zwick's hard-hitting, Academy Award-winning American Civil War drama *Glory* (1989).

In the nineties, Broderick's career diversified still further, with many appearances in film and on television. He starred alongside screen legend Marlon Brando in Andrew Bergman's organised crime comedy *The Freshman* (1990), and appeared in romantic comedies such as Warren Leight's The *Night We Never Met* (1993) and Alan Parker's eccentric historical comedy-drama *The Road to Wellville* (1994). He had also a high-profile comic role as the beleaguered Steven Kovacs, the foil for Jim Carrey's sinisterly hyperkinetic cable TV technician, in Ben Stiller's *The Cable Guy* (1996). Broderick further stretched his dramatic muscles in biographical drama *Infinity* (1996), which he was also to direct, based upon the life of the Nobel-prize winning American physicist Richard Feynman. His star profile also remained assured at the end of the decade following appearances in popular films including Roland Emmerich's ambitious remake of *Godzilla* (1998), and Alexander Payne's pithy satire *Election* (1999). He made a move into family features with an appearance as John Brown, better known as *Inspector Gadget*, in David Kellogg's 1999 film of the same name, and also as the voice behind Simba in Disney's perennially popular *The Lion King* (1994), directed by Roger Allers and Rob Minkoff. Broderick reprised the role of Simba in Darrell Rooney and Rob LaDuca's *The Lion King II: Simba's Pride* (1998), and again later in Bradley Raymond's *The Lion King 11/2*

(2004).

In more recent years, Broderick's prolific screen career has shown no signs of slowing down. He appeared in Kenneth Lonergan's harrowing, Academy Award-nominated drama *You Can Count on Me* (2000), Tom Cairns's surreal *Marie and Bruce* (2004) (adapted from a stage play by Wallace Shawn), and Jeff Nathanson's knockabout comedy *The Last Shot* (2004). He starred in Frank Oz's high-profile remake of *The Stepford Wives* (2004), and made an appearance in Paul Dinello's satire *Stangers with Candy* (2005). However, by far his most prominent performance of the past decade, in terms of public awareness, came in 2005 with his appearance as nervous accountant Leopold Bloom in Susan Stroman's *The Producers* (2005), a musical remake of Mel Brooks's classic 1968 comedy, where Broderick was to reprise his role from the show's massively successful Broadway run. Nearer the end of the decade, he continued to divide his time between comedies such as John Whitesell's *Deck the Halls* (2006) and Terry Kinney's *Diminished Capacity* (2008), comedy-dramas like Helen Hunt's *Then She Found Me* (2007) and Peter Tolan's *Finding Amanda* (2008), and more serious dramatic roles in films such as Joshua Goldin's *Wonderful World* (2009) and Kenneth Lonergan's *Margaret* (2010). His voice acting has also continued successfully in films including Steve Hickner and Simon J. Smith's *Bee Movie* (2007) and Sam Fell and Robert Stevenhagen's *The Tale of Despereaux* (2008).

Broderick has received and been nominated for a number of awards over the years. These included a nomination for an Emmy Award (Outstanding Supporting Actor in a Miniseries or a Special) for his appearance as John in Gregory Mosher's television drama *A Life in the Theater* (1993), adapted by David Mamet from his own stage play. He was nominated for a Golden Globe Award for his performance as Ferris Bueller in *Ferris Bueller's Day Off*, and also received a Saturn Award nomination for his starring role in *WarGames*. Additionally, he was nominated for a Tony Award (Best Actor in a Musical) for his performance in the stage version of *The Producers* in 2001. In 2006, he and his co-star from *The Producers*, Nathan Lane, laid a star on the Hollywood Walk of Fame in a double ceremony.

ALAN RUCK (Cameron Frye)

Although in his late twenties by the time he made his breakthrough into cinema, Alan Ruck's youthful appearance allowed him to make memorable appearances as teenage characters in films such as Rick Rosenthal's drama *Bad Boys* (1983) and Lewis John Carlino's romantic comedy *Class* (1983). He had also appeared in television dramas including Peter Werner's *Hard Knox* (1984) and Sheldon Larry's *First Steps* (1985). After appearing as Cameron Frye in *Ferris Bueller's Day Off*, Ruck continued to divide his time between appearances on both film and television. His cinematic work included supporting performances in comedies which included Bill L. Norton's *Three for the Road* (1987), Francis Veber's *Three Fugitives* (1989) and Howard Brookner's *Bloodhounds of Broadway* (1989).

In the nineties, Ruck continued to diversify his cinematic career while making increasingly prolific appearances on television. He appeared as Hendry William French in Geoff Murphy's western drama *Young Guns II* (1990), as Dean in Mark Halliday and Bram Towbin's *Just Like in the Movies* (1992), and played Stephens in Jan de Bont's popular, high-octane action thriller *Speed* (1994). He established his cult credentials with an appearance as Captain John Harriman, the immediate successor to Captain James T. Kirk as commander of the Starship Enterprise, in David Carson's *Star Trek: Generations* (1994). Although his appearance in the film was relatively brief, Ruck would reprise the role – and greatly expand upon it – thirteen years later in Tim Russ's ambitious independent film *Star Trek: Of Gods and Men* (2007). Later in the decade, Ruck made appearances in films such as John Gray's family drama *Born to Be Wild* (1995), Jan de Bont's natural disaster thriller *Twister* (1996), Matt Mulhern's contemplative *Walking to the Waterline* (1998), Steven Cantor's complex mockumentary *Endsville* (2000), and Marc Forster's *Everything Put Together* (2000). On television, Ruck appeared in shows as diverse as *Tales From the Crypt* (1993), *The Outer Limits* (1996) and *Mad About You* (1995-96). However, on TV he was best-known by far for his appearance as regular character Stuart Bondek in ABC's *Spin City* (1996-2002).

The rate of his television performances has remained constant in recent years, with appearances in many shows including *Scrubs* (2002), *Medium* (2007), *Ghost Whisperer* (2007), *Boston Legal* (2008), *FlashForward* (2009), *Cougar Town* (2009) and *CSI: Crime Scene Investigation* (2010).

Most recently, Ruck's cinema performances have included comedies such as Shawn Levy's *Cheaper By the Dozen* (2003), Daniel Schechter's socially-conscious drama *Goodbye Baby* (2007), Matthew Miele's inventive, complex *Eavesdrop* (2008), and Robert Dyke's science fiction thriller *InAlienable* (2008). He continues to remain very active in both film and television, with appearances in high-profile features including M. Night Shyamalan's mystery thriller *The Happening* (2008), David Koepp's zany supernatural comedy *Ghost Town* (2008), and Tom Vaughan's medical drama *Extraordinary Measures* (2010).

MIA SARA (Sloane Peterson)

Mia Sara's first film role, which immediately preceded her appearance in *Ferris Bueller's Day Off*, was in Ridley Scott's fantasy adventure *Legend* (1985), opposite Tom Cruise and Tim Curry. Following her performance as Sloane Peterson, Sara divided her time between television and film. Her cinematic career in the eighties included Tom Clegg's action drama *Any Man's Death* (1988), Ralph L. Thomas's crime mystery *Apprentice to Murder* (1988), and Terrell Tannen's atmospheric thriller *Shadows in the Storm* (1988). Her television work included dramas such as Larry Peerce's *Queenie* (1987) and Jan Egleson's *Big Time* (1989), in addition to appearances in television series such as *Alfred Hitchcock Presents* (1988) and *Till We Meet Again* (1989).

Sara continued to work in both film and television throughout the nineties. Her film appearances included features such as J.S. Cardone's suspense thrillers *A Climate for Killing* (1991) and *Black Day Blue Night* (1995), Sidney Lumet's romantic drama *A Stranger Among Us* (1992), Scott McGinnis's crime mystery *Caroline at Midnight* (1994), and Peter Hyams's science fiction action movie *Timecop* (1994). Later in the decade, her performances continued with George Mihalka's action thriller *Bullet to Beijing* (1995), Strathford Hamilton's high-tech drama *The Set Up* (1995), Danny Huston's intense horror *The Maddening* (1996), Richard Schenkman's wry romance *The Pompatus of Love* (1996), and David Lister's family comedy *Dazzle* (1999). Meanwhile, her work for television blended appearances in series such as *Time Trax* (1993), *Strangers* (1996) and *Chicago Hope* (1995-96) with TV dramas including Stuart Gordon's *Daughter of Darkness* (1990), Thomas Michael Donnelly's *Blindsided* (1993), Eric Red's *Undertow* (1996), Rod Hardy's adaptation of Jules Verne's *20,000 Leagues Under the Sea* (1997), and Burt Reynolds's *Hard Time* (1998).

Since the turn of the century, Sara's appearances have been less prolific. She has had roles in Charles Jarrott's crime drama *Turn of Faith* (2001), Martin Wood's family adventure *The Impossible Elephant* (2001), Ashley Way's Great Depression-set comedy *Hoodlum and Son* (2003), and Leigh Scott's fantasy *The Witches of Oz 3D* (2010). Her television performances have included Brian Henson's family drama *Jack and the Beanstalk: The Real Story* (2001) and Mick Garris's lively fantasy *Lost in Oz* (2002), as well as television shows such as *CSI: NY* (2005), *Nightmares and Dreamscapes* (2006) and *Tinseltown* (2007). She has also provided voice work for films such as Gregory Gieras's *Little Insects* (2000), and as Dr Harleen Quinzel (better known as Harley Quinn) in Warner Brothers' short-lived Batman-related animated series *Birds of Prey* (2002-03). Sara won the 1995 Saturn Award for Best Supporting Actress in recognition of her role as Melissa Walker in *Timecop* (1994).

JEFFREY JONES (Edward Rooney)

Jeffrey Jones's successful career as a character actor began in the 1970s with an appearance in Paul Williams's militaristic drama *The Revolutionary* (1970). He performed on television throughout the decade, alternating between dramatic productions including Peter Levin's American Civil War drama *Secret Service* (1977) and Martin Hoade's thriller *Interrogation in Budapest* (1978), and appearances in TV series such as *Sara* (1976) and *Kojak* (1977). Jones's career continued to alternate between film and television throughout the eighties, where he was often to be found playing oddball eccentrics and intense antagonists. He was cast as the U.S. Secretary of Defence in James Glickenhaus's suspense thriller *The Soldier* (1982), as Clive Barlow in James Signorelli's comedy *Easy Money* (1983), which starred Rodney Dangerfield and Joe Pesci, and also as Lepescu in Rudy De Luca's horror spoof *Transylvania 6-5000* (1985). However, he was perhaps best-known to audiences at the time for his scene-stealing performance as the foppish dilettante Emperor Joseph II in Milos Forman's ground-breaking biographical drama *Amadeus* (1984).

Following his appearance in *Ferris Bueller's Day Off*, Jones would continue to move between comedic and dramatic roles, including Dr Walter Jenning in Willard Huyck's comic book fantasy *Howard the Duck* (1986), Fischer in Lionel Chetwynd's dark Vietnam War drama *The Hanoi Hilton* (1987), and the hapless Charles Deetz in Tim Burton's *Beetle Juice* (1988). He also played Inspector Lestrade alongside Michael Caine's Sherlock Holmes in Thom Eberhardt's lively crime satire *Without a Clue* (1988), and Gercourt in Milos Forman's *Valmont* (1989), an adaptation of Choderlos de Laclos's classic novel *Les Liaisons Dangereruses*, as well as Eliot Draisen in Paul Flaherty's entertaining farce *Who's Harry Crumb?* (1989), appearing opposite John Candy. His prolific television work in the eighties included Hal Cooper's romantic comedy *A Fine Romance* (1983), Jerry London's mystery drama *If Tomorrow Comes* (1986), and perhaps most memorably his appearance as Thomas Jefferson in William A. Graham's biographical drama *George Washington II: The Forging of a Nation* (1986). He also appeared in television series as wide-ranging as *Remington Steele* (1983), *The Twilight Zone* (1985) and *Amazing Stories* (1986).

In the nineties, he remained a prominent supporting actor in many high-profile films such as John McTiernan's Tom Clancy adaptation *The Hunt for Red October* (1990) and Greg Beeman's family comedy *Mom and Dad Save the World* (1992), while he delivered a note-perfect performance as unconventional continuity announcer Criswell in Tim Burton's unforgettable biopic *Ed Wood* (1994). Later in the decade, he was to appear as Thomas Putnam in Nicholas Hytner's *The Crucible* (1996), a big-screen adaptation of the famous Arthur Miller play, and as Eddie Barzoon in Taylor Hackford's occult legal thriller *The Devil's Advocate* (1997). His versatility as a performer was particularly evident at the end of the nineties, when he was cast in very diverse roles over a short period of time: in one year, he was to alternate between the cannibalistic horror of Antonia Bird's *Ravenous* (1999), Tim Burton's fantasy-based mystery *Sleepy Hollow* (1999), and Rob Minkoff's hit family comedy *Stuart Little* (1999).

Jones's television performances in the nineties included appearances in series including *Tales from the Crypt* (1993) and *The Outer Limits* (1998), as well as in TV dramas such as Craig R. Baxley's western thriller *The Avenging Angel* (1995). He also provided an impressive amount of voice acting for animated series such as *Duckman* (1994), *Batman: The Animated Series* (1995) and *Eek the Cat* (1996), as well as President Richardson in Interplay's wildly successful role-playing videogame *Fallout II* (1998).

More recently, he has appeared in a variety of film comedies which include Peter Askin and Douglas McGrath's *Company Man* (2000), David Mirkin's *Heartbreakers* (2001), Jesse Dylan's *How High* (2001), Steve Carr's *Dr Dolittle 2* (2001), and Grant Heslov's *Par 6* (2002). On television, he made appearances in Randall Miller's acerbic family-based comedy *Till Dad Do Us Part* (2001) and in an episode of *Trailer Park Boys* (2004), while also providing voice work for animated series such as *Justice League* (2002) and in various episodes of *Invader ZIM* between 2001 and 2006. He played the prominent regular role of A.W. Merrick in HBO's western drama *Deadwood* (2004-06), and also appeared recently in Don Michael Paul's sporting film comedy *Who's Your Caddy?* (2007).

For his performance in *Amadeus*, Jones was nominated for a Golden Globe Award (Best Performance by an Actor in a

Supporting Role in a Motion Picture) in 1985. He was also nominated, along with the rest of the cast of *Deadwood*, for the Outstanding Performance by an Ensemble in a Drama Series Award at the 2007 Screen Actors Guild Awards.

JENNIFER GREY (Jeanie Bueller)

Jennifer Grey's career in cinema began with her appearance as Cathy Bennario in James Foley's romantic comedy-drama *Reckless* (1984). This was quickly followed by performances in John Milius's Cold War action adventure *Red Dawn* (1984), Francis Ford Coppola's period crime drama *The Cotton Club* (1984) and John Badham's sporting drama *American Flyers* (1985). She also had television roles in two instalments of *ABC Afterschool Specials* between 1984 and 1985. However, it was following her performance in *Ferris Bueller's Day Off* that she made what was to be almost certainly her best-known film appearance of the eighties as Frances 'Baby' Houseman in Emile Ardolino's celebrated romantic drama *Dirty Dancing* (1987), alongside Patrick Swayze.

In the early nineties Grey's acting career centred mainly upon television, with appearances in gritty crime dramas such as Roger Young's *Murder in Mississippi* (1990), Andy Wolk's *Criminal Justice* (1990), Peter R. Hunt's *Eyes of a Witness* (1991) and Duncan Gibbins's *A Case for Murder* (1993). Her other television roles during the decade included parts in Tom Clegg's Cinderella-inspired *If the Shoe Fits* (1990), Ernest Thompson's stage adaptation *The West Side Waltz* (1995), Mark Piznarski's drama *The Player* (1997), Robert Allan Ackerman's intense thriller *Outrage* (1998), and David Schwimmer's romantic comedy *Since You've Been Gone* (1998). She also made appearances in long-running television series such as *Friends* (1995) and *Fallen Angels* (1995). Grey's cinematic performances throughout the nineties included roles in Carroll Ballard's sailing drama *Wind* (1992), Bill Corcoran's legal drama *Portraits of a Killer* (1996), Peter Shaner's comic romance *Lover's Knot* (1996), and Allison

Burnett's challenging emotional drama *Red Meat* (1997).

She has continued to be active in film since the turn of the century, appearing in romantic dramas such as Don Roos's *Bounce* (2000) and Todd Kessler's *Keith* (2008), Avi Nesher's horror *Ritual* (2001), and David Mamet's martial arts drama *Redbelt* (2008). Grey has also engaged with a number of television performances in recent years, with roles in features including Mark Jean's festive family comedy *Road to Christmas* (2006), TV series such as *John from Cincinnati* (2007) and *The New Adventures of Old Christine* (2009), and voice acting in the animated series *Phineas and Ferb* (2008-09).

Grey was nominated for a Golden Globe Award for Best Performance by an Actress in a Motion Picture (Comedy/ Musical) in 1988 for her appearance in *Dirty Dancing*.

SUPPORTING CAST

Lyman Ward (Tom Bueller) has been a prolific actor since the early 1970s, with performances in many high-profile television series including *Bonanza* (1971), *Laverne and Shirley* (1976), *Kojak* (1977) and *Battlestar Galactica* (1979). He has played a number of supporting roles over the years, becoming more active in the film world throughout the course of the eighties with roles in features such as Amy Holden Jones's dark thriller *Love Letters* (1983), Paul Mazursky's comedy drama *Moscow on the Hudson* (1984) and Jack Sholder's fantasy horror *A Nightmare on Elm Street Part 2: Freddy's Revenge* (1985). However, he was better known throughout that decade for his varied television appearances in series as diverse as *Cagney and Lacey* (1982), *Dallas* (1985), *The A-Team* (1986), *Magnum P.I.* (1987), *She's the Sheriff* (1987) and *Family Ties* (1989). Ward's prolific output continued into the nineties, with roles in films which included Mick Garris's horror thriller *Sleepwalkers* (1992), Penelope Spheeris's comedy remake *The Beverly Hillbillies* (1993), and Roland Emmerich's science fiction blockbuster *Independence Day* (1996). At the same time, his television appearances included parts in series such as *Beverly Hills 90210* (1990), *Melrose Place* (1993), *Weird Science* (1994) and three different roles in *Murder, She Wrote* between 1991 and 1995. Although less prolific in recent years, Ward has continued to remain active in film and television, with cinematic roles in features such as Joel Gallen's satire *Not Another Teen Movie* (2001), Mark Jones's crime thriller *Quiet Kill* (2004), and Jonah Salander's drama *Privileged* (2010). His television appearances in the past decade have included episodes of *Black Scorpion* (2001), *J.A.G.* (2001 and 2003), and *Monk* (2008).

Cindy Pickett (Katie Bueller) first appeared on television in the late 1970s, and was quickly to establish herself both in film and on TV. Her varied cinematic performances included roles in Roger Vadim's sensual drama *Night Games* (1980), Andre R. Guttfreund's romance *Breach of Contract* (1982), Chris Bearde's comedic horror *Hysterical* (1983), Peter Medak's relationship-based drama *The Men's Club* (1986), and Sean S. Cunningham's science fiction thriller *DeepStar Six* (1989). Additionally, she appeared in many television dramas throughout the decade, such as Kieth Merrill's *The Cherokee Trail* (1981), Jackie Cooper's *Family in Blue* (1982), Donald Wrye's *Amerika* (1987), and Lesli Linka Glatter's *Into the Homeland* (1987). Pickett also played regular characters in *Call to Glory* (1984-85) and *St Elsewhere* (1986-88), as well as making appearances in other long-running series throughout the decade. In the nineties, she played parts in TV series which included *L.A. Law* (1992), *Murder, She Wrote* (1994) and *Sirens* (1995), with a recurring role in *Hyperion Bay* (1998-99). As well as appearing in TV dramas such as Mel Damski's western thriller *Wild Card* (1992) and Dan Lerner's *Her Hidden Truth* (1995), Pickett also appeared in cinematic roles in films which included Steve Rash's comedy *Son in Law* (1993), Mark Rosman's science fiction action thriller *Evolver* (1995), and Matias Alvarez's rodeo drama *Coyote Summer* (1996). Since the turn of the century, she has alternated between appearances in TV series such as *NYPD Blue* (2005), *CSI Miami* (2005), *Cold Case* (2007) and *Burn Notice* (2009), and film roles such as Tommy Stovall's thriller *Hate Crime* (2005), Daniel Waters's romantic comedy *Sex and Death 101* (2007), Chris J. Ford's thoughtful drama *The Village Barbershop* (2008), and EdK's crime thriller *Confession* (2010).

Edie McClurg (Grace the Secretary) has been a highly prolific performer on television and film throughout the years, starting with voice acting on Hanna-Barbera's *The Jetsons* (1962). Her cinematic debut was in Brian De Palma's Stephen King adaptation *Carrie* (1976), and from there she has remained active in supporting roles ever since. Her television appearances have included roles in *The Chevy Chase Show* (1977), *W.K.R.P. in Cincinnati* (1979-80), *The Pee-wee Herman Show* (1981), *Diff'rent Strokes* (1984), *Moonlighting* (1986), *The Golden Girls* (1991), *Roseanne* (1992), *Full House* (1992), *Seinfeld* (1993), *Picket Fences* (1996), *Touched by an Angel* (1997), *Married with Children* (1997), *Columbo* (1998), *Mad About You* (1999), *Caroline in the City* (1998-99), *CSI: Crime Scene Investigation* (2005) and *Days of Our Lives* (2009), amongst a great many others. Her vocal performances have ranged across animated series as varied as *Scooby-Doo and Scrappy-Doo* (1979), *TaleSpin* (1990), *Darkwing Duck* (1991), *Tiny Toon Adventures* (1991), *Goof Troop* (1992), *Batman Beyond* (2000) and *The Life and Times of Tim* (2008 and 2010). Her many film appearances have included Rowby Goren and Chuck Staley's disaster movie parody *Cracking Up* (1977), Alfred Sole's comedic horror *Pandemonium* (1982), Tommy Chong's cult comedy *Cheech and Chong's The Corsican Brothers* (1984), John Hughes's travel comedy *Planes, Trains and Automobiles* (1987), Robert Redford's historical drama *A River Runs Through It* (1992), Les Mayfield's fantasy remake *Flubber* (1997), Walt Becker's lively romantic comedy *Van Wilder* (2002), Mark Edwin Robinson's mystery thriller *Breaking Dawn* (2004), and David A.R. White's religious satire *Holyman Undercover* (2010).

Ben Stein (The Economics Teacher) has become immortalised in popular culture for his droning, tongue-in-cheek performance in *Ferris Bueller's Day Off*, and prior to Hughes's film he had made only one other cinematic performance, in Art

Linson's teen comedy *The Wild Life* (1984). In addition to acting he has had a very diverse career, having worked in the legal industry, in academia, as a Presidential speech-writer, and as an acclaimed journalist for many newspapers and magazines, including *The Wall Street Journal*. He has also published a large number of novels and non-fiction books. Following his *Ferris Bueller's Day Off* appearance, he has performed widely in films, on television series and dramas, and in commercials. His cinematic work has included Ivan Reitman's fantasy sequel *Ghostbusters II* (1989), Andrew Bergman's romantic comedy *Honeymoon in Vegas* (1992), Nick Castle's comic book adaptation *Dennis the Menace* (1993), David Frankel's humorous romance *Miami Rhapsody* (1995), Chuck Russell's frenetic action fantasy *The Mask* (1994) and its sequel, Lawrence Guterman's *Son of the Mask* (2005). He has appeared in television series such as *The Wonder Years* (1989-91), *MacGyver* (1991), *Tales from the Crypt* (1995), *Lois and Clark: The New Adventures of Superman* (1995), *Seinfeld* (1997), *Murphy Brown* (1997), *Muppets Tonight* (1998) and *The Drew Carey Show* (2001). He has also been a hard-working voice actor, providing performances in series including *Duckman* (1996-97), *Rugrats* (1998), *Pinky and the Brain* (1998), *King of the Hill* (2004), *The Emperor's New School* (2006-08) and *Family Guy* (2003 and 2009). Between 1997 and 2002, Stein also hosted a highly successful TV game show entitled *Win Ben Stein's Money*, for which he was awarded a Daytime Emmy in 1999. He was nominated for the same award again in 2001, 2002 and 2003.

Kristy Swanson (Simone Adamley) only had a brief appearance in *Ferris Bueller's Day Off*, but it was just the beginning of a long-running career that had started with a cameo in another John Hughes-scripted film, Howard Deutch's *Pretty in Pink* (1986), and a variety of dramatic roles on television such as *Cagney and Lacey* (1985) and *Alfred Hitchcock Presents* (1986). Since then, she was to appear in films such as Wes Craven's tongue-in-cheek horror *Deadly Friend* (1986), Jeffrey Bloom's mystery thriller *Flowers in the Attic* (1987), Tom Logan and Hugh Parks's teen fantasy *Dream Trap* (1990) and Jim Abrahams's parody of air force movies, *Hot Shots!* (1991), before delivering one of her best-remembered performances in the title role of Fran Rubel Kuzui's *Buffy the Vampire Slayer* (1992). Her later film roles included John Singleton's education drama *Higher Learning* (1995), Tony Spiridakis's crime thriller *Tinseltown* (1997), Dennis Dugan's comedy-drama *Big Daddy* (1999), Danny Leiner's larger-than-life action comedy *Dude, Where's My Car?* (2000), Tom Whitus's crime mystery *Silence* (2003), and Dallas Jenkins's romantic drama *What If...* (2010). On television, she has played roles in series including *Knots Landing* (1987-88), *Nightingales* (1989), *Early Edition* (1998-99), *Grapevine* (2000), *Just Shoot Me!* (2003), *CSI: Miami* (2004), *Law and Order: Criminal Intent* (2007), and *One Tree Hill* (2010). Swanson won a Young Artist Award (Best Young Actress: Guest in a Television Series) in 1986 for her early appearance in *Cagney and Lacey*, and was nominated for Young Artist Awards again in 1987 (Exceptional Young Actress Starring in a Television Special or Movie of the Week) for her part in Oz Scott's comic horror *Mr Boogedy* (1986); in 1988 (Best Young Female Superstar in Motion Pictures) for her performance in *Deadly Friend*, and in 1989 (Best Young Actress in a Horror or Mystery Motion Picture) for her role in *Flowers in the Attic*.

Charlie Sheen (Boy in Police Station) may have only appeared in a brief cameo in *Ferris Bueller's Day Off*, but at the time he was already well established in the world of film, having appeared in features which included John Milius's *Red Dawn* (1984), Penelope Spheeris's *The Boys Next Door* (1985) and David Seltzer's *Lucas* (1986), as well as a number of TV dramas. He went on to major cinematic success later in the eighties, appearing in critically and commercially successful films which included Oliver Stone's *Platoon* (1986) and *Wall Street* (1987), and Christopher Cain's *Young Guns* (1988). In the nineties he continued to diversify, which films such as Lewis Teague's military action film *Navy Seals* (1990), Jim Abrahams's knowing spoof *Hot Shots!* (1991) and its sequel *Hot Shots! Part Deux* (1993), Stephen Herek's literary adaptation *The Three Musketeers* (1993), Deran Sarafian's thriller *Terminal Velocity* (1994), Albert Pyun's mystery drama *Postmortem* (1998), and Spike Jonze's magnificently surreal *Being John Malkovich* (1999). In recent years he has become just as well-known for his television performances, including regular roles as Charlie Crawford in *Spin City* (2000-02) and as Charlie Harper in *Two and a Half Men* (from 2003). His cinematic appearances since the turn of the century have included Steve Rash's romantic comedy *Good Advice* (2001) and George Armitage's crime thriller *The Big Bounce* (2004), while he reprised his role as Bud Fox in Oliver Stone's *Wall Street* sequel, *Money Never Sleeps* (2010). His many awards have included four nominations for the Outstanding Lead Actor in a Comedy Series Emmy Award between 2006 and 2009, and two nominations in 2005 and 2006 for the Best Performance by an Actor in a Television Series (Musical or Comedy) Golden Globe Award, for his long-running performance in *Two and a Half Men*. In 2002 he won a Golden Globe Award for Best Performance by an Actor in a Television Series (Musical or Comedy) for his highly-successful role in *Spin City*. He has also been nominated for a Screen Actors Guild Award in 2000 (as part of the ensemble cast of *Being John Malkovich*) and again in 2005 and 2010 (for his lead performance in *Two and a Half Men*). In 1994 the achievements of his career were recognised with a star on the Hollywood Walk of Fame.

(Please note that the dates given above for television series refer to the actors' specific appearance on a particular episode of the named TV show, rather than the full duration that the series was in production.)

3

FERRIS BUELLER'S DAY OFF

THE LOCATIONS

In the years since its release, Ferris Bueller's Day Off *has come to be particularly well-known as a visual travelogue of Chicago, a city that was close to the heart of John Hughes. Like many of his films, it makes extensive use of the urban sophistication and rural beauty of the state of Illinois, which forms the film's backdrop. This chapter takes a look at the locations that were used throughout* Ferris Bueller's Day Off. *Some are famous, a few will seem familiar from their appearance in the film, and others aren't quite what they appear to be.*

THE BUELLER FAMILY HOME

Although Ferris Bueller's upmarket home is one of the main locations in the film, it is unusual amongst the other featured venues in that it is situated not in Illinois, but in California. The building is a private residence, located at Country Club Drive, Long Beach, Los Angeles, CA 90807. Hughes implies within the narrative of the film that the house is sited within the Chicago suburbs, possibly in the fictional Shermer district where the later scenes in the nearby police station take place, and which also features throughout earlier Hughes films such as *The Breakfast Club*.

OCEAN PARK HIGH SCHOOL

Ferris's *alma mater* is actually Glenbrook North High School, which is located at 2300 Shermer Road, Northbrook, IL 60062. It first opened in 1953, and is still a working fouryear high school today. Glenbrook North High School has long been renowned for its high teaching standards, and was visited in 1997 by then-incumbent U.S. President Bill Clinton, who gave a high-profile speech on education there.

Visit the website:
http://www.glenbrook225.org/north/Pages/default.aspx

THE FRYE FAMILY HOME

The distinctive residence of the Frye family is a private home located on Beech Street, Highland Park, IL 60035. The beautiful leafy ambience of the area, which is suggested in the film, is still in evidence there today.

THE MULTI-STOREY CAR PARK

When Ferris, Cameron and Sloane leave Mr Frye's Ferrari in a downtown multi-storey car park for the duration of their stay in Chicago, they may have been interested to know that the building would still be fulfilling the same function well over two decades later. The car park is owned by General Parking Corporation, and is located on West Madison Street & Wells Street, Chicago, IL 60606.

Visit the website:
http://chicago.citysearch.com/profile/37830925/chicago_il/general_parking_corporation.html

THE SEARS TOWER SKYDECK

One of the most instantly recognisable of all Chicago landmarks, the Sears Tower – now officially renamed the Willis Tower, as of July 2009 – stands 442m high, making it one of the top five tallest buildings on the planet. It is located at 233 South Wacker Drive, Chicago, IL 60606. In the film, Ferris and his friends look down upon the city from the building's famous observation area, the Skydeck.

Visit the website:
http://www.theskydeck.com/

THE CHICAGO BOARD OF TRADE

Ferris, Cameron and Sloane watch the fevered trading in the Chicago Board of Trade from the comparative tranquillity of its visitor centre. Situated at 141 West Jackson Boulevard, Chicago, IL 60604, the Chicago Board of Trade has been based in its current building since 1930 (though the organisation itself was established long beforehand, in 1848). Standing 184m high, its distinctive architecture and National Historic Landmark status make it a prominent sight within Chicago's Loop district.

Visit the website:
http://www.cbot.com/

THE ART INSTITUTE OF CHICAGO

This significant fine art museum was held in high esteem by Hughes, so it is no surprise to see Ferris and his friends spending some time there during their day off. Located at 111 South Michigan Avenue, Chicago, IL 60605, the Art Institute of Chicago has a vast number of holdings in its extensive collections, including artworks from across the globe and from many periods in history. The second largest art museum in America, it has received particular acclaim for its world-class collections of Impressionist artwork. Amongst the Institute's treasures are Georges Seurat's *Sunday Afternoon on the Island of La Grande Jatte* (which mesmerises Cameron in the course of his visit), and numerous paintings by Monet, Renoir, Toulouse-Lautrec and Cézanne. It is also home to Grant Wood's famous *American Gothic*.

Visit the website:
http://www.artic.edu/

THE VON STEUBEN DAY PARADE

It's a total stroke of luck for Ferris that his visit to Chicago should happen to coincide with the famous Von Steuben Day parade. Taking place along the city's centrally-located Dearborn Street, this celebration is customarily held midway through the month of September to commemorate the life of Baron Friedrich von Steuben. The event is observed in many large American cities (most especially New York City), with Chicago's parade being organised by the United German-American Societies of Greater Chicago. Established in 1957, the event celebrated its 50th anniversary in September 2007.

Visit the website:
http://www.germanday.com/

THE CHEZ QUIS RESTAURANT

The memorably snooty maitre d' of the Chez Quis restaurant would no doubt have been scandalised to learn that his establishment was never an upmarket eating place at all. Rather, it is a private residence based in West Schiller Street, Chicago, IL 60610. Carefully redressed for the scenes in which it appeared, the exterior of the house has been extensively redesigned since the filming of *Ferris Bueller's Day Off*.

WRIGLEY FIELD BASEBALL STADIUM

The home of the famous Chicago Cubs since 1916, Wrigley Field is located at 1060 West Addison Street, Chicago, IL 60657. One of the best-known professional sporting locations in the city, as it has been for several decades, this baseball stadium is the oldest National League ballpark and has a seating capacity of 41,160.

Visit the website:
http://www.mywrigleyville.com/

4

FERRIS BUELLER'S DAY OFF

THE MUSIC

There are few who would argue that John Hughes was a director who really loved music. His films in the mid-eighties featured a meticulously-selected assortment of tracks which perfectly epitomised the cultural ambience of the time. Yet unusually for a Hughes teen movie, no original soundtrack for Ferris Bueller's Day Off *was ever officially released. The director's diverse choice of musical styles combined to create one of the most eccentric – and memorable – collections of songs and melodies ever to grace a Hughes feature. Because of the enduring cult success of* Ferris Bueller's Day Off, *many of the songs have since come to be closely associated with the film. What follows is a list of the most prominent tracks to feature throughout the course of the film.*

LOVE MISSILE F1-11

One of the first songs to be heard in the film, 'Love Missile F1-11' was performed by Sigue Sigue Sputnik, an acclaimed British synth-pop band which has been active since the mid-eighties. It was written by Tony James, Neil Whitmore & Martin Degville. The song has become one of the band's most recognisable tracks, and was released to considerable acclaim (it reached number three in the UK Singles Chart) in 1986. 'Love Missile F1-11' has been covered by other artists, most notably by Pop Will Eat Itself in 1987.

JEANNIE (THEME FROM *I DREAM OF JEANNIE*)

Written by Hugo Montenegro, this sprightly piece of music was composed for the muchloved American situation comedy *I Dream of Jeannie*, which ran from September 1965 to May 1970. It starred Barbara Eden (in the title role) and Larry Hagman, and was produced for five seasons totalling 139 episodes. Its whimsical tone suited the series perfectly, and will be instantly recognisable to many American TV viewers and admirers of vintage comedy.

OH YEAH

'Oh Yeah' was written and performed by Boris Blank and Dieter Meier, better known as Yello. The fondly-remembered electronica band, hailing from Switzerland, was probably best-known for this particular song, and as soon as it struck up (upon the first appearance of Mr Frye's Ferrari) it was instantly to pass into popular lore. It can also be heard at the end of the film, playing over the credits as Ed Rooney faces the agonising humiliation of hitching a ride on a school bus full of bemused students. The distinctive song's popularity was such that it came to be used in a number of other high-profile films throughout the eighties, including Rod Daniel's *Teen Wolf* (1985), Herbert Ross's *The Secret of My Success* (1987), George Costello's *K-9* (1989), and Stan Dragoti's *She's Out of Control* (1989).

BEAT CITY

The perfect accompaniment to Ferris's victorious arrival in Chicago, this song plays as Hughes treats the viewer to a rapid-fire, MTV-style succession of images showing the bustling city in motion. It was written and performed by The Flowerpot Men, also known as Ben Watkins and Adam Peters, who were active in the eighties and originated in the UK. 'Beat City' was almost certainly their most well-known song. The Flowerpot Men were later to change their band's name to Sunsonic, under which they would produce several other songs.

MENUET CÉLÈBRE

Heard playing in the upmarket Chez Quis restaurant, the famous Menuet Célèbre is taken from Luigi Boccherini's String Quintet in E Major, Op. 11, No. 5. Boccherini (1743 -1805) was an Italian composer best known for the above String Quintet and his Cello Concerto in B flat major. In *Ferris Bueller's Day Off*, the menuet in question is being played by the Zagreb Philharmonic Chamber Studio.

BAD

Written by Mick Jones and Don Letts, 'BAD' was performed by Big Audio Dynamite, a British group formed in the early eighties. Their most prominent member was Mick Jones, who had previously been a singer and guitarist with The Clash. This song was one of their best-remembered from the decade, though they were to produce many other tracks throughout the eighties.

STAR WARS (MAIN TITLE)

Heard when the audience become aware of the sheer exuberance of the joyriding taking place in Cameron's father's Ferrari, this iconic piece of music is immediately familiar not only to fans of science fiction films, but to any self-respecting cinema-goer since the seventies. It was composed by John Williams, who has scored many of the top grossing box-office hits of the film world over the past several decades (including many of Steven Spielberg's most successful movies, such as the four *Indiana Jones* films, *Jurassic Park*, and *E.T.: The Extra Terrestrial*). Williams has been nominated for Academy Awards on no fewer than forty-five occasions, and has won five Oscars to date as well as a great many other prestigious awards. This celebrated theme, performed by the London Symphony Orchestra, is almost certainly the most immediately identifiable within the *Star Wars* films, and occurs in the opening credits of all six features in the cycle.

PLEASE PLEASE PLEASE LET ME GET WHAT I WANT

Written by Steve Morrissey and Johnny Marr, this song was originally performed by The Smiths, one of the most significant British alternative rock bands of the eighties. Heard during the Art Institute of Chicago sequence, the version of the song used in *Ferris Bueller's Day Off* was a cover by The Dream Academy, an English folk rock band who were active throughout the decade. 'Please Please Please Let Me Get What I Want' can also be heard in another well-known Hughes production, Howard Deutch's *Pretty in Pink* (1986). The song has been covered by many other artists, among them Hootie and the Blowfish, Kate Walsh, The Halo

Benders, and Amanda Palmer.

DANKE SCHOEN

Ferris sings this song at the Von Steuben Day Parade in Chicago and, earlier in the film, while having a morning shower. It was first performed by Bert Kaempfert, who also composed the song (with lyrics written by Kurt Schwaback and Milt Gabler) in 1962. However, the version of the song to which Ferris is miming during the parade is actually performed by Wayne Newton in 1963, and is considered by most to be the definitive rendering. Newton has enjoyed a highly successful career from the sixties onwards, and is particularly well-known for his famous live performances in Las Vegas. 'Danke Schoen' is, for many, the most recognisable song of his long career, having become almost synonymous with the artist.

TWIST AND SHOUT

A true classic of early rock 'n' roll, 'Twist and Shout' was written by Phil Medley and Bert Russell. It was originally recorded by the Top Notes, but was famously covered by The Beatles in 1962. The song was released on The Beatles' first album *Please Please Me* and was released as a single in the United States in March 1964. It is The Beatles version of the song which appears in *Ferris Bueller's Day Off*, forming the latter half of Ferris's parade float performance. It has been covered a great many times over the years by several different bands and artists, and is considered by some to be one of The Beatles' most significant early tracks.

I'M AFRAID

Written by David Joyner & Paul Mansfield, 'I'm Afraid' was performed by Blue Room. The band were no strangers to John Hughes productions; their song 'Cry Like This' was performed in Howard Deutch's *Some Kind of Wonderful* (1987), while 'Everytime You Go Away' was to appear in the later *Planes, Trains and Automobiles* (1987).

RADIO PEOPLE

'Radio People' was the fourth track on *The New Zapp IV U*, the fourth studio album by Ohio-based band Zapp, which was released in 1985. The song was written by Larry Troutman and Terry 'Zapp' Troutman. Zapp was an influential band at the time, especially on the American West Coast, and was formed in 1978 by five brothers: Larry Troutman, Terry Troutman (better known as 'Zapp'), Lester Troutman, Tony Troutman and Roger Troutman. They had a number of successful hits which included 'Computer Love' and 'More Bounce to the Ounce'.

TAKING THE DAY OFF

This song was performed by General Public, a rock band which was active between 1984 and 1995. General Public was formed by Ranking Roger and Dave Wakeling, artists formerly of The Beat. 'Taking the Day Off' was written by David Wakeling.

THE EDGE OF FOREVER

This is the second song to appear in the film which was performed by The Dream Academy, a band which consisted of instrumentalist Kate St John, keyboard player Gilbert Gabriel, and lead singer and guitarist Nick Laird-Clowes. Whereas the earlier 'Please, Please, Please Let Me Get What I Want' had been presented as an instrumental track in the film, 'The Edge of Forever' was included as a vocal track.

MARCH OF THE SWIVELHEADS

Heard as Ferris makes his epic race to reach home before his family, 'March of the Swivelheads' was an instrumental remix of the song 'Rotating Head'. Both songs were written and performed by British ska band The Beat (sometimes known outside the UK, particularly in North America, as The English Beat). Often engaging with issues of culture and ideology in their music, The Beat formed in 1978 and were to release three albums in the early 1980s.

5

FERRIS BUELLER'S DAY OFF

SCENE BY SCENE ANALYSIS

When Ferris Bueller's Day Off *first went on general release in America during the summer of 1986, audiences were presented with one of the most multifaceted and structurally refined of all John Hughes's films. In this section, I will take a detailed look at the way in which Hughes carefully constructs this well-loved movie, examining the skilful manner that he employs irony, wit and inspired characterisation in order to densely permeate his narrative with many distinctive contrasts and rewarding connections.*

John Hughes chooses to begin *Ferris Bueller's Day Off*, inventively enough, not with an image but a line of dialogue from a breakfast radio broadcast. Against a dark background, we are told not only that the weather is favourable, but also where the action is going to be situated – the Chicago area. This is followed soon after by the voice of Ferris Bueller's mother Katie repeatedly trying to wake her son and, when he doesn't respond, calling out for her husband Tom. As she does so, the opening credits (still being shot on a dark background) suddenly give way to a wide-angle shot of the Bueller family home – a location which is pivotal throughout the course of the film.

As we hear Tom running upstairs to his son's room, we see Ferris for the first time. He is lying in bed, open-eyed but apparently comatose. A concerned Katie explains that although Ferris claims not to have a fever, he is feeling unwell. Ferris then claims to have difficulty recognising Tom, further fuelling his parents' concerns. Katie notes that Ferris's hands are cold and clammy – a notion which Tom puts to the test. But after he does so, Ferris makes an apparently laboured attempt to get out of his bed. Tom and Katie are alarmed, given the symptoms he has outlined to them, but Ferris is insistent, claiming to have a test at school that he doesn't want to miss.

Here we see Ferris's reverse psychology at work for the first time – by trying to convince his parents of his profound sense of responsibility, even in the face of illness, he hopes to persuade them of the seriousness of his condition. Even as he emphasises his concern that he doesn't want to put his chances of attending a decent college at risk, Tom and Katie are determined that he not leave his 'sick bed'.

We then meet his sister Jeanie, introduced by close-up shots of her impatiently tapping feet in trainers, and her hands resting on her hips in an assertive fashion. The cynicism of Jeanie's tone of voice clashes with the earnestness of her parents' obvious concern. She is unimpressed by Ferris's performance, and totally unconvinced of his malaise – even when he tries an even more ostentatious demonstration of his lack of depth of vision after she enters the room. He does, however, risk a cheeky wink to her – unseen by his parents – which inflames her temper even further. Jeanie rails at the injustice of Ferris's attempt to evade his classes, claiming that even if she were at death's door her parents would insist on her attendance at school. Ferris weakly chides her, telling her to be grateful that she is still in good physical condition. But this time he pushes the envelope still further, giving her a signal of mock-secrecy by theatrically putting his finger to his lips. Obviously as intended, Jeanie is outraged, though she barely manages to contain her indignation. With one final barb at her parents, she storms out.

With the introduction of Jeanie, Hughes presents the lesser of the film's two ostensible antagonists, and also sets up the sibling rivalry which exists between this unconventional brother and sister act. Jeanie's hot temper is made evident, as is Ferris's innate sense of playful deceit. He also lays out the beginning of their shared antipathy which plays out during the day ahead – Jeanie's grievance at the injustice of Ferris's seemingly-effortless duping of their parents, and the danger of Ferris's scheming being exposed by Jeanie.

With Jeanie's departure, Ferris continues to ramp up the intensity of his bedridden performance to his parents. Katie, and then Tom, both assure Ferris that they'll keep in regular touch with him even while they're at work during the day. Ferris pours on the sentiment, thanking them for being such kind and considerate parents. They accept his dying swan routine without question, so convincing do they find his alleged ailments, and they even seem reluctant to depart from his side. The minute that Tom and Katie leave the room, however, Ferris sits bolt upright in bed and – addressing the camera directly – revels in the fact that he's managed to fool them so successfully.

There follows a montage from MTV, shown on Ferris's television set, before the camera returns to Ferris himself once again. Still talking directly to camera, he voices incredulity that his parents were so easily fooled when he considered his presentation to be – compared to earlier performances – relatively poor. Triumphantly, he throws back the curtains to his bedroom, and asks why anyone should want to be in high school on such a day. To prove his point, we are then presented by a beautiful blue sky soaring above leafy green trees. Lively music begins to strike up in the background. Returning to Ferris, we can plainly see a look of unadulterated exultation spreading over his face.

As he adjusts the equaliser of his impressive-looking hi-fi system, Ferris explains to the audience that this has been the ninth day of absence that he has managed to engineer during the current semester, and laments the difficulty of having to present new and diverse forms of illness. As he points out, he'd have to go all-out for a tenth day, and is thus determined to make the most of this day away from school.

We move next to a wide-angle shot of Ferris's bedroom, which provides a good panorama of his plentiful (and eclectic) collection of belongings. Taking a relaxed seated position, Ferris gives the audience a primer on how to fool their parents into giving them the day off. His points are represented onscreen with superimposed captions. First, he recommends clammy hands – an unfocused kind of symptom that is difficult to diagnose. However, he advises against a bogus fever, warning that it can lead to parents seeking a medical opinion – never a good thing. As he talks, Ferris is tying a sports trophy to a length of string, but offers no explanation for his action. (This will become relevant later.)

Next, he provides his sick-day masterplan: simulate a stomach cramp, lean over holding your abdomen while giving vocal expression to your pain, and then give your palms a lick. As he points out, even although it may appear a puerile scheme, it is no more infantile than the school you're trying to avoid. Then, as he leaves his room to walk down the hall to the bathroom, he delivers one of the film's most iconic lines, informing the audience that life is so fast-paced that – every once and again – they should make sure that they stop to appreciate it before it's gone forever.

Already, less than five minutes into the film, we have been introduced to a great deal of what makes Ferris such an appealing character. Although wilfully cunning and devious, he is also charming and charismatic. His attitudes are both life-affirming and vaguely philosophical, albeit in a playful way. We know that not only is he a past-master at getting his own way, not least with regard to his attendance at school, but also that he is both meticulous in his planning and contemplative in his approach to life. We will see ample evidence of these two traits later.

Ferris gets out of his bathrobe and, in a tastefully framed shot, has a shower. Having sculpted his hair into a Mohican style with shampoo, he assures the audience that he wasn't lying about having a test at school – he really did have one scheduled – but as the topic was European socialism, he saw little point in participating. As he points out, seeing that he has no interest in ever becoming European, the inhabitants of that continent can follow whatever political model that pleases them – it isn't a big issue to him, unlike the fact that he doesn't have his own car. (Ferris's lack of a car of his own is quite possibly the most major irritant in his life, and here Hughes provides the first indication of it.) He then switches from a fixed shower-head to a mobile one, bursting into song as he rinses himself off (and playfully covering his face to mock-protect his identity).

Back in the upstairs hallway, his hair and lower body shrouded by towels, Ferris adds a small caveat to his earlier pronouncement about European politics. He says that he doesn't feel that allowances should be made for extreme political systems, regardless of nationality, but instead believes that people should believe in themselves rather than in ideologies. But at any rate, as he points out, none of this changes the fact that he still needs to sponge a ride in other people's cars because he has no transport of his own.

We then suddenly switch to Ferris's alma mater, Ocean Park High School, where his economics teacher is droningly going through the class register. Various students respond to their names – vocally or by gesture – as he tediously goes through the roll-call. When he reaches Bueller on the register, there is no response – yet even although Ferris's desk is clearly empty, the teacher continues to repeat his name in the same monotonous tone of voice. One of Ferris's classmates points out that she has heard on the grapevine that Ferris is ill, having passed out at a café the night beforehand. The teacher thanks her, but is so monumentally dull and expressionless that it is not entirely clear whether he believes this account or not. Next on the register is Frye – a name which the teacher again reads out repeatedly, but to no response.

Hughes uses a very effective switch in tone here, moving from Ferris's upbeat, confident assertions of the importance of liberty to the school's comparatively oppressive environment, as suggested by his economics teacher's repetitive droning. The muted colours of the school are in stark contrast to the vibrancy and eclecticism of Ferris's home, and the audience is left in absolutely no doubt that Ferris – even before his day has really started – is indisputably enjoying himself more than his semi-catatonic fellow students. It is a skilful comparative distinction that is used several times throughout the film.

The next shot is of an upmarket residence surrounded by tall green trees. Upon moving inside the house, the first image that greets the viewer is of an expensive-looking multi-function telephone surrounded by various small bottles of medicine. A hand is feebly lowered from the side of a bed to engage the speakerphone. An equally weak voice asks who is calling: the person on the other end of the line is indistinguishably Ferris. Ferris's voice reveals who we are being introduced to: his closest friend, Cameron Frye. We then move back to see Cameron's room in its entirety; it almost looks like a kind of high-tech mortuary, with closed curtains framing his bed in the foreground, a couple of small mirror-balls suspended from the ceiling, and a plasma globe mounted on a pedestal nearby. Ferris enquires after his friend's health. Cameron responds that he is feeling very unwell, and when asked about the whereabouts of his mother replies that she is currently away from home. As their conversation continues, a number of additional shots provide further glimpses of medicine bottles lying around, and various other malady-related paraphernalia including what appears to be a mixed cold cure in a glass (not yet drunk) and a box of paper tissues on Cameron's beside cabinet.

In a complete change of ambience, we then suddenly switch to a relaxed Ferris – still holding the conversation with Cameron, a cordless phone in his hand – as he suns himself on a garden lounger. He is now wearing Hawaiian-style beach shorts and sipping a cocktail from an ostentatious-looking receptacle. Ferris tries to cajole his friend into coming over, explaining that he's taking the day off. However, Cameron – who genuinely does seem to be unwell – refuses. But Ferris won't take no for an answer, apparently not because he wants Cameron's company so much as for the reason that his friend has his own car. Hughes continues to repeatedly move between Ferris's carnivalesque corner of his back yard and the sombre appearance of Cameron's sickbed. Ferris rings off, frustrated, but then calls back again immediately afterwards to convince Cameron that he isn't really unwell, just unimaginative – there is so much more to do than lying around in bed.

In a sense, Hughes is using this scene to foreground the major issues which will later confront Cameron; the character is hidebound by neuroses which Ferris compels him to deal with as the day continues. As Ferris explains to camera, he is keen to assist Cameron in becoming less repressed and self-conscious before he leaves high school, so that he will better be able to appreciate college. This is juxtaposed with an image of Cameron, still in bed, wallowing in self-pity.

The audience next find themselves in a leafy commercial area. Moving closer, we see that our location is a realtor agency, Koenig and Strey. Inside, Katie is at her desk in a plush communal office area. She is answering her phone, on the other end of which is Edward R. Rooney, the dean of students at Ferris's high school. Katie's soft but professional phone manner is immediately contrasted with Rooney's officiously pompous tone. Katie is apologetic, as she had intended to call the school to inform them of Ferris's absence. There is then an establishing shot of the school exterior, with a running student (presumably late for class) in the background and a couple of parked bicycles in the foreground. As Rooney presses the issue, asking Katie if she is aware that Ferris is not present at school, we move inside the school to see a variety of students departing at high speed to their respective classes, save for one hapless character who has dropped a loose-leaf folder and is now surrounded by piles of random sheets of paper. As Katie again apologises for not having been in touch, we are introduced to Rooney's eccentric secretary Grace, who is deep in thought at her desk. Without warning, she produces a pencil out of her hair. She then stops, confused, and pulls out another pencil. And another. Rooney, meanwhile, is emphasising his disdain for Ferris's record of attendance at school. He stresses to Katie his concern that Ferris has not been paying adequate attention to his studies. We then move to Rooney's desk, upon which lies a highly-polished nameplate. Any immediate effect of impressiveness that this is meant to convey is slyly undermined by Hughes with the placement of a half-eaten packet of indigestion tablets next to the nameplate. (Hughes may be underscoring Rooney's uptight nature here even before we see the character himself – could it be that Rooney's constant irritation has already led him to develop a peptic ulcer?)

As Rooney flicks a tiny speck of dirt from the edge of his desk, the audience gets their first look at the film's main antagonist. Still on the phone, he explains to Katie that Ferris has now been absent from school on nine occasions during the current semester. Rooney takes great pleasure in telling Katie that, if he is not fully satisfied by Ferris's academic performance, he will not hesitate in forcing her son to repeat his current year of high school. Katie is surprised at this news, but Rooney is insistent – he has checked the school's computer database, which holds the school's attendance details. As Katie continues to voice her disbelief, punctuated by Rooney needling her with his scepticism over Ferris's honesty (or perceived lack of it), he continues to search for further miniscule fragments of grit or dust scattered around his desk. A shot at another angle shows his office to be fastidiously tidy, perfectly reflecting his anally-retentive obsession with methodical order. Rooney, now becoming indignant, stresses the fact that no matter how Katie may refuse to accept the fact, Ferris really has been absent on nine separate occasions. However, as he makes this declaration, he watches in shock as the number on the monitor screen before him is reduced in front of his eyes from nine down to two days of absence.

Switching back to Ferris's bedroom, we can see the same record being displayed on Ferris's home computer (an IBM PCjr). As Ferris points out, he may not have a car, but a computer – while not as useful on a day to day basis – does have some uses. (His skill at network hacking marks a neat tip of the hat to Matthew Broderick's well-received performance in John Badham's *WarGames* (1983), where he played a teenage computer expert who breaks into the U.S. government's defence network and very nearly manages to trigger World War III by accident.)

Back at the school, Rooney is apoplectic. He repeatedly calls for his secretary Grace with mounting vehemence, but cutting back to her desk we can see that she is currently occupying herself by sniffing a bottle of correction fluid. While Rooney continues to furiously call out to Grace, his hand momentarily covering the receiver's mouthpiece, Katie calmly explains to him that while some students may well feel inclined to bunk off school at certain times of the year, she is absolutely convinced of Ferris's ill-health, so much so that she even debated taking the day off herself to look after him. As she says this, we cut back to Ferris – still in his bedroom – as he blows tunelessly on a clarinet. He claims never to have taken any lessons; from his musical performance, it's unlikely that anyone would disbelieve this fact.

This is the first example of Ferris managing to outsmart Rooney, and with considerable aplomb. Although Rooney, with all his overbearing self-importance, believes himself to be in a position of absolute primacy at the school, Ferris will continue to undermine his self-satisfied sense of authority as the film progresses.

In the economics class, the teacher is giving a mind-bogglingly dull appraisal of the 1930 Hawley-Smoot Tariff Act. Although he makes some token attempts to engage class participation, all of the students appear on the verge of falling into a coma by his colossally boring style of delivery. Shots of the teacher hovering in front of his blackboard are intercut with brief portraits of the staggeringly uninterested students, one of whom has fallen asleep in a puddle of his own saliva. We then suddenly cut to Ferris at home who, in sharp contrast, is blithely dancing around in a Hawaiian shirt, striped trousers and Converse trainers. Once again, the distinction could not be more apparent.

Jeanie is walking down a bustling high school corridor, bag over arm, when a friend catches up with her and expresses her regret over Ferris's condition. When Jeanie – irritated – asks why she thinks that he's ill at all, the friend explains that it's an issue that is being widely talked about. Apparently one of the fellow students in her biology class has become convinced that Ferris, should his condition worsen and eventually kill him, wants to donate his eyes to Stevie Wonder. Jeanie is quietly incensed by Ferris's popularity among the student body at large, and his seemingly-effortless ability to con virtually everyone that he meets. Another friend then approaches Jeanie, but – now more sullen than ever – she brushes her off and wanders out of shot. As Jeanie does so, she reveals a group of younger male students using a payphone in the background.

It transpires that the students are calling Ferris to ask about his condition. Ferris explains that he is still in a poor way – a fact which he 'proves' with the inventive use of an electronic synthesiser (an E-MU Emulator II) which has been loaded with various samples of coughing, sneezing and other sounds of general malaise. The students are relieved to know that Ferris is still alive, not least as he has promised one of them that he'll help them to trick their way out of summer school. They then pass the phone on to a passing female student, who also asks after Ferris's health. Ferris responds with an ever-more ostentatious collection of ailing body sounds, claiming that he may need a kidney transplant to ensure his recovery. The female student seems saddened by this, but brightens up when Ferris tells her that he'll probably still be alive at the weekend – she hopes to catch up with him then. Ferris thus perpetuates the now near-mythic reputation of the gravely poor condition of his health amongst the student body at large. Returning to Ferris's bedroom, we find him performing a rather unorthodox rendering of Johann Strauss's 'Blue Danube' waltz on his synthesizer keyboard, replete with a variety of snorts and sniffles.

In the dean's office, Rooney is going through a huge pile of paper printouts – presumably hard-copies of attendance records. He tells Grace of his manifest distrust of Ferris, voicing his concern that the miraculous Bueller ability to pull the wool over the eyes of authority will have a corrosive effect on the rest of the school. Rooney is disturbed by the thought of having to deal with a legion of students duplicating Ferris's schemes, as it will hamper his ability to run the school efficiently. And, as Grace helpfully pipes up, it will inevitably make him look even more stupid than Ferris has already done. In spite of Rooney's protestations, Grace continues by saying that the key to Ferris's success is his popularity – he is respected by all of the school's diverse cliques, regardless of age, gender or social background. That, asserts Rooney, is why he absolutely needs to prove without any possibility of doubt that Ferris has been lying to the school and to his parents, thus putting a stop to his free-wheeling disrespect for authority. Grace then unwittingly plays into Rooney's considerable vanity, comparing the intensity of his anti-Ferris diatribe to that of Clint Eastwood's eponymous hero in Don Siegel's *Dirty Harry* (1971). Rooney responds to this with a magnificently ham-fisted attempt at an Eastwood-esque snarling expression, though his demonstration appears totally lost on Grace.

Back in his bedroom, Ferris is on the phone to Cameron trying to cajole him to get out of bed and drive over. As Ferris speaks, we can see that he is using a mouse to sketch a picture of a naked woman with a graphic design package on his computer. Switching over to Cameron, who is now sitting up in bed, there seems to be little difference from his earlier appearance. He insists that his blood pressure reading is unfavourable and that he has no intention of leaving his bed. But Ferris becomes ever more adamant. Pointing out that he'll be lucky to graduate from high school if he's caught truanting, and is unlikely to have the same golden opportunity presented to him again, he is determined to make this day off count. He is interrupted by another call, which turns out to be from his father Tom. Instantly affecting an ailing tone of voice, Ferris answers the call. We then move to an establishing shot of a busy commercial sector of Chicago, followed by the interior of Tom's upmarket office. His desk appears splendidly lavish. Tom is still concerned for Ferris's wellbeing, particularly as he sounds no better than when he left home in the morning. Quickly switching back to his conversation with Cameron, Ferris warns his friend to get over with his car as soon as possible. Then returning to his father's call, he claims that the conversation is making him dizzy and that he should be returning to bed. Tom recommends that he take a hot bath, swathe his head with a hot towel, and then make some soup before getting some sleep. Ferris tells his dad that he loves him before hanging up and returning to converse with the camera. He laments the fact that Cameron seems to have let him down, and speculates that by now he will probably be sitting in his car agonising over whether he should stay at home or acquiesce to his friend's wishes.

True enough, we then move to a medium close-up of Cameron in the driver's seat of his car. And equally true is the fact that he is torturing himself over what course of action to take.

Talking to himself, he comes to the conclusion that disagreeing with Ferris will only delay the inevitable, as his friend is unrelenting in the pursuit of his aims and never loses an argument. Though he is monumentally frustrated at being so obviously manipulated, punching the front passenger seat in irritation, he revs the engine and prepares to depart. And then changes his mind. Moving to a camera position some distance further away, a shot which takes in both his car and the exterior of his residence, Cameron removes his seatbelt and gets out of the car. Then, returning to the medium close-up of the driver's seat view, we watch as he casts around in rage, his movements just visible from the car's rear window.

Here Hughes reveals more of Cameron's character, juxtaposing his sense of inner repression with his loyalty to Ferris – and, of course, his unconscious longing for the kind of liberation that Ferris's artful scheming represents. Ultimately, the audience already knows – as Cameron probably does – that he will eventually go along with his friend's machinations, irrespective of his misgivings.

We move next to an English literature class, where another deathly dull teacher – who has a stilted, almost staccato means of delivery – is lecturing his class. A wide shot of his class reveals, on the extreme right of the frame, Ferris's girlfriend Sloane Peterson. Like the rest of her classmates, she appears bored rigid. There is then a cut to a pair of legs adorned with neatly creased white trousers and neat white shoes, striding purposefully down a school corridor. Panning up, we are introduced to a school nurse, wringing her hands as though anxious about something. Cutting back to Sloane, who is now yawning with boredom, the English teacher is continuing to drone on with his lecture. He is interrupted when the nurse arrives via the classroom's main doorway. Before the nurse has even had a chance to explain her purpose there, Sloane is already in the process of putting on her jacket. The nurse calls out for her, and Sloane affects an exaggerated look of total surprise. Moving back out of the classroom, Sloane and the nurse head down the corridor together. The nurse delicately explains to Sloane that her father has called the school to explain that her grandmother has unexpectedly passed away. Sloane appears distraught (almost comically so, under the circumstances), and the nurse does her best to comfort her.

Although at this point we are unaware of Sloane's identity, or indeed her relevance to the film, her humorously calculating actions presage her relationship with Ferris and her complicity with his elaborate schemes. (Also germane is the fact that we later learn that the nurse is called Florence Sparrow, a play on the name of the eminent historical nurse of the Crimean campaign, Florence Nightingale.)

In Ed Rooney's office, Grace is explaining that she'd taken the aforementioned phone call from Sloane's father, and has asked the nurse to inform Sloane of the death in the family. Rooney immediately smells a rat, and asks Grace who Sloane is currently dating. When Grace replies that she often sees Sloane and Ferris together, Rooney becomes certain of foul play. He asks Grace to find Sloane's father's phone number, but before she has the opportunity to do so she takes an incoming call... which turns out to be from none other than George Peterson himself. Rooney, however, is convinced that rather than Sloane's father, Ferris is on the other end of the line impersonating him. Taking the call, Rooney feigns sympathy when 'George' asks for Sloane to be excused from class, but then demands to have sight of the grandmother's dead body before he'll release Sloane from school. Grace is stunned by Rooney's callousness and enquires about his uncaring approach to the conversation, but Rooney assures her that he's merely setting a snare to trap Ferris into revealing his attempt at deception. However, a second incoming line then rings on Grace's desk; Ferris is calling in to speak to Rooney. Alarmed, Grace runs back into Rooney's office and gesticulates wildly. Annoyed, Rooney asks what the matter is, only to be told that he's not in fact speaking to Ferris at all. A hilariously dramatic jarring chord, coupled with a tight focus on Rooney's alarmed expression, underscores the monumental depth of his gaffe.

Switching to the second line, Rooney listens as Ferris crisply explains that as he is currently absent from school, he wonders if Jeanie might possibly pick up any class-related work for him so that he can catch up on any assignments before his return.

Rooney is too shocked to answer, his expression growing ever more distressed. After Ferris hangs up, Rooney switches back to 'George'. Immediately apologetic, he meekly expresses regret for his earlier insensitivity. But 'George' is furious at Rooney's lack of consideration. We then cut back to Ferris's house, where 'George' is actually revealed to be Cameron (wearing, appropriately enough, a T-shirt bearing a medical caduceus). As Cameron cranks up the irritation that Sloane's father would likely be feeling at the earlier slight, Rooney becomes tongue-tied with apprehension. He frantically signals Grace to find out what class Sloane is in so that she can be released from school for the day. However, while Grace and Rooney have difficulty in finding the information they need, Cameron begins to overplay his hand. Ferris, now sharply dressed, assures Cameron that his performance is impeccable, even though his friend is starting to lose his nerve. On the other end of the line, Grace impersonates Rooney while the dean agitatedly rifles through notes in an attempt to pin down Sloane. As Rooney returns to the phone receiver, Cameron demands that Sloane be sent out to the front of the school so that he can pick her up. Ferris is concerned that this will look suspicious, so Cameron improvises and tells Rooney to accompany Sloane to the car. Ferris is now getting worried, and slaps Cameron to quickly persuade him to change the plan. Ad-libbing frantically now, Cameron ends the call by telling Rooney that he's changed his mind – he doesn't have time to talk, but will get back in contact later so that the two of them can have lunch together.

These scenes underscore not only Ferris's continuing and innate ability to run rings around Rooney (and, by extension, the school system), but also Rooney's inflated perception of his own ability to smoke out Ferris's conniving plans. His dawning horror at his supposed error of mistaken identity, coupled with his Keystone Kops-style slapstick antics as he tries in vain to pin down the paperwork he needs to locate Slone, articulate much about the way that his character thinks and operates.

Back in Ferris's painstakingly ordered kitchen, Cameron is annoyed at Ferris for having slapped him. Now calm, Ferris explains that they will have difficulty extracting Sloane from the school if Rooney is watching them too intently. But Cameron is irritated with Ferris for not only manoeuvring him into leaving his home and driving over to the Buellers' house, but also for having asked him to make a fake call to Rooney's office (not least considering the potentially disastrous consequences if things had gone wrong). Infuriated at Ferris's lack of respect for his feelings, Cameron grabs his jacket and moves to walk out of the house. Ferris, however, turns on the charm and manages to talk Cameron out of a hasty departure.

At the school, Rooney is racing down one of the corridors, comically slowing down as he passes every doorway so as to conceal his urgency from any student who might happen to see him. Cutting back to the Buellers' kitchen, Ferris and Cameron have now made amends. However, Ferris explains that because picking up Sloane has now been made a much more potentially hazardous undertaking, he will require Cameron to supply a little something extra in order to make his plan work.

Moving then to Cameron's father's garage, we watch as the camera pans up from Ferris and Cameron's feet to their heads as they gaze in awe at the sight that awaits them. That sight is then revealed to be an extremely rare 1961 Ferrari 250GT California – Mr Frye's pride and joy, which he has spent years restoring to a state of perfection. On our first view of the car, the distinctive sound of Yello's song 'Oh Yeah' (1985) strikes up. As Cameron underscores his father's absolute devotion to this vehicle, the audience is treated to several lingering close-ups of various parts of the car's bodywork, including shots of the distinctive Ferrari emblem. Although there are other vintage cars in the attractive glass-panelled garage, the Ferrari is clearly in pride of place. Ferris moves over to assume a posing position near the Ferrari as he explains to Cameron that he intends to take the car out of the garage to pick up Sloane. Cameron is horrified at the prospect, and frantically tries to talk Ferris out of the scheme while his friend – in love with the very sight of the car – wanders around it to take in the full extent of its splendour. In spite of Cameron's grave misgivings, not least at the almost certain ire of his tyrannical father, Ferris is insistent. He explains that Rooney will never accept that George Peterson would drive a banged-up old car like Cameron's, and that only arriving in the Ferrari will convince him that the situation is a believable one. Cameron is resolutely opposed to the idea, but by now Ferris is in the driver's seat and raring to go. Cameron pleads with him, saying that his father will notice that the odometer will have increased with every mile that they've travelled, but Ferris brushes off his concern, explaining that they'll leave the car in reverse gear later so as to reduce the figures on the odometer. But while Cameron crosses himself and makes one last desperate attempt to talk Ferris out of his plan, offering to rent a Cadillac or hire a limousine instead, Ferris is already driving out of the garage, stopping just long enough to let Cameron into the car.

Mr Frye's Ferrari, perhaps the single most prominent visual symbol in the film, represents not only his avaricious acquisitiveness, but also the disciplinary powers that he ruthlessly wields over his son Cameron. Although Hughes has already established Cameron's hypochondria and slightly neurotic nature, we are somehow left in no doubt from his reactions in this scene that his father's fury will potentially be severe indeed. Nor indeed do we have any hesitation in believing Cameron's account that the ownership and condition of the car really does mean more to him than his son.

Eagle-eyed members of the audience will note that the Ferrari's numberplate reads 'NRVOUS', appropriate given Cameron's state of mind throughout most of the film. The other main characters' cars also bear numberplates that are made up of abbreviated titles from earlier Hughes films. Ed Rooney's car is designated '4FBDO' ('For *Ferris Bueller's Day Off*'), while Jeanie's is 'TBC', after *The Breakfast Club*. Even Ferris's parents get in on the act; Tom's car bears a 'MMOM' (*Mr Mom*) numberplate, while Katie's reads 'VCTN' (*National Lampoon's Vacation*).

Rooney is accompanying Sloane out of the school's main doorway as they await the imminent arrival of her 'father'. From inside the school, Jeanie is watching the situation unfold at a distance. Rooney is now exaggeratedly apologetic after his earlier faux-pas, and quotes from the Old Testament (Job 14:1-2) in a rather surreal attempt to comfort her. However, as Sloane does not respond to his attempts at conversation, the exchange becomes increasingly strained and awkward. A school bus passes by, suddenly revealing Mr Frye's Ferrari behind it. Standing in front of the car is a heavily-disguised Ferris (complete with dark glasses, long overcoat and hat). He calls out for Sloane, thus avoiding having to get near enough to Rooney to face close scrutiny, and fortunately Rooney seems not to notice that the voice of 'George' sounds nothing like it had done during their earlier phone conversation. Sloane pauses only to thank Rooney for his empathy and consideration, inflating his already considerable sense of self-importance, before she heads for the car.

Jeanie is watching all of this from the main school doors, situated just behind Rooney. The droning voice of the economics teacher is just audible in the background. From her expression, we can tell that she is quietly exasperated by the fact that Ferris has managed to pull the wool over the school's eyes yet again.

At the side of the Ferrari, Sloane greets Ferris with a long, lingering kiss on the lips. As their embrace becomes ever more intimate, Rooney looks on with increasing discomfort. He purses his lips in distaste at what appears to be an incestuous clinch between the two. Ferris and Sloane get into the car, and Sloane inconspicuously greets Cameron, who is concealed in the back. When she asks Ferris what his plans are, he reveals that he has ambitious aspirations for the day ahead – much to Cameron's alarm, as he is still massively apprehensive about the use of his father's car. Ferris revs the engine and speeds off into the distance, with Sloane cheering for joy. Still standing at the school doorway, Rooney is beginning to look suspicious.

Here we see that Sloane, now united with Ferris, is of the same mind with regard to the blundering school authorities, effortlessly buttering up Rooney while maintaining (at least initially) the ostensible appearance of a grieving teenager. Rooney's hilariously clumsy attempts to be both apologetic and comforting, on the other hand, are skilfully contrasted with his dawning mistrust of the situation as it unfolds.

Now free from the watchful eye of Rooney, Ferris continues to accelerate as they head down the road from school. Cameron, deciding that he can risk exposing his presence, unearths himself from the back of the car. Ferris triumphantly tosses his hat into the air as Cameron – almost drowned out by the sound of the engine – begs him to slow down.

We are next greeted with a panoramic establishment shot of the Windy City of Chicago. Soaring skyscrapers and busy traffic are evident everywhere. Hughes then shifts to a variety of more detailed shots, some showing well-known Chicago buildings and landmarks. Highly distinctive architecture can be seen in this variety of stunning aerial shots. Eventually, we move back to the Ferrari as it speeds along a road heading into the city. Ferris is still riding the car hard. We switch next to a viewpoint directly in front of the car, as though staring through the windscreen. Without audible dialogue, Cameron is chiding Ferris for not decelerating, and Ferris responds by repeatedly taking his hands off the wheel, predictably causing Cameron to freak out.

Back in high school, a student is collecting donations in an empty cola can as he walks along a corridor. Many passing teenagers rattle coins into the can as they go by. That is, until he meets Jeanie. When she asks what he is collecting for, the student explains that he is helping to raise money in order to purchase Ferris a new kidney. Enraged, Jeanie knocks the can flying out of his hand and storms off. Mystified by her seemingly-heartless actions, the student asks her what she'll do if she ever needs help from Ferris Bueller in the future. Jeanie predictably offers no response.

Grace is dialling the Peterson's home telephone number at Rooney's request. Rooney, meanwhile, is now back at his desk and looking increasingly distrustful. As he lifts the receiver to connect to his extension line, we cut to Sloane's answering machine at her home. Her recorded message plays a tearful message explaining the details of their family bereavement, and also outlines a separate contact number. Rooney explains to Grace that he is now sure that there is a ruse at work, that Ferris is behind it, and that Sloane is implicated. (And, as Grace asks to Rooney's disdain, can we be sure that Sloane's grandmother isn't also mixed up in it somehow?) When the further contact number is dialled, it connects to Cameron's answering machine, which plays a message purporting to be from a mortician. Rooney, now convinced of foul play, tells Grace that he is absolutely determined to uncover Ferris's deception and make him face the consequences of his actions.

Rooney's attitude in this scene is interesting, as he makes a conscious shift from simply seeking to bring Ferris to book, penalising him for not respecting school rules, and instead he begins to develop a personal obsession with pursuing his dispute with Ferris. No longer hoping simply to catch him out, Rooney is now upping the ante considerably, unwavering in his resolve to damage Ferris's future by curtailing his perceived subversive ambitions.

Ferris has now slowed down somewhat as the car has reached inner-city Chicago. He turns into a multi-storey car park, where he intends to leave the Ferrari for the day. Cameron is alarmed by this, knowing that if the car is even slightly damaged he could face major ramifications at home. But Ferris is persistent, stressing that he'll tip the valet to ensure that no harm comes to Mr Frye's pride and joy. The valet soon arrives, clocking in, and Ferris approaches him with a rather indiscreet enquiry about his language skills. The man responds in heavily-accented English that yes, he does indeed speak the same language. (With an ironic glance to camera, we can see that Ferris is not entirely convinced of this.) Ferris hands over his tip, asking the valet to take particular care of the Ferrari. Cameron is extremely reluctant to leave the vehicle, but is eventually persuaded out by Ferris and Sloane. The valet assures him that he has no cause for concern, before carefully driving the car further into the building. Yet just as Cameron is coaxed out onto the city street by his friends, the Ferrari can be seen – entirely unobserved by Ferris and associates – screeching out of the car park, with the valet in the driving seat and one of his colleagues along for the ride. They are then witnessed racing off into the city at high speed.

These scenes set up the source of a major predicament later in the film – any change in the Ferrari's status, now out of Ferris's control, is bound to have major negative consequences for Cameron. Yet in a more understated way, it also delineates a certain subtle degree of xenophobia on Ferris's part. His rather insensitive questioning of the valet, fundamentally about his nationality, calls to mind his earlier comments about having no interest in the affairs of other countries, their politics or their respective mindsets.

Back at the Buellers' house, Katie is returning to check on Ferris. Parking in the driveway, she quietly enters the house and – as suspenseful music plays – gently creeps upstairs as not to disturb her son. Slowly opening the door to Ferris's room, she looks in to see a gently turning figure in bed. The light sound of contented snoring can also be heard. Satisfied, she closes the door, but reminded of Rooney's earlier warning about excessive absences she feel compelled to have another quick glance. As she does so – though unseen by Katie – the apparatus of Ferris's deception is laid bare. The sporting trophy, which he was seen tying up earlier in the film, is suspended behind the door to act as a counterweight. Through a complex system of strings and pulleys, when the door opens the trophy's suspension is slackened, causing a mannequin (concealed under a quilt) to turn in Ferris's bed. Meanwhile, a looped track of snoring samples is being played on his hi-fi. Still apparently satisfied by her son's apparent infirmity, Katie closes the door behind her for a second time and heads downstairs.

In Chicago, Ferris, Sloane and Cameron are on the observation level of the Sears Tower. Ferris is revelling in being at the top of the highest building on the planet; Cameron, still worried about the Ferrari, is feeling distinctly vertiginous. Taking pleasure in the moment, Ferris invites his friends to stand higher on the observation rail and rest their heads against the glass of the windows. This gives each of them an even more arresting view of the city below. Sloane is amazed at how tranquil Chicago looks from her current height. Cameron, on the other hand, is convinced that he can see his father.

Here Hughes again emphasises the psychological differences between Ferris and Sloane, both obviously deriving gratification in their distant observation of the world below, and Cameron, whose paranoia over his father's inescapable disparagement is inhibiting his ability to let himself unwind even remotely.

The action then briskly moves to the floor of the Chicago Board of Trade, where a horde of traders can be seen frenetically dealing in commodities. This frantic scene is intercut with a view of Cameron apparently giving some brokeresque hand-signals. Eventually it becomes apparent that he, Sloane and Ferris are all sitting within a sealed-off observation area, with the traders some distance away behind a wall of glass. Ferris half-jokingly asks Sloane if she'll consider marrying him during the course of the day. Sloane laughs his offer off, asking him to think about the profound ramifications of what he's asking. Cameron, making annoying noises with his cheeks, glumly cuts across the conversation to interject that his own parents are a perfect demonstration as to why the institution of marriage is futile. As he points out, his mother and father may be married, but they also hate each other. In Cameron's opinion, his father loves his Ferrari, but detests his own wife. Yet Ferris and Sloane do not appear to let their friend's sense of resentment towards his parents dampen their own romantic sanguinity.

Cameron here demonstrates once again the clear difference between his own bleak outlook on the future, and the much more upbeat prospects that Sloane and Ferris have in mind. The scene also serves to further elaborate upon Cameron's miserable home life, underscoring the fact that his mother is at least as much at variance with Mr Frye as Cameron himself is.

Next we see an exterior shot of Chez Quiz, an upmarket restaurant in the city. Moving inside, Ferris and friends are waiting in a high-class reception area, grossly underdressed amongst the other sharply-attired guests. Ferris surreptitiously checks the reservations list before the arrival of a snooty maitre d', who is instantly suspicious of the three teenagers. The maitre d' asks if Ferris has made an advance booking, to which Ferris responds that he has made a reservation for a party of three under the name of Abe Froman – having seen the name on the maitre d's own list. However, the maitre d' is unimpressed. In his opinion, Abe Froman – 'The Sausage King of Chicago' – would clearly look nothing like a casually-dressed teenager. Ferris, however, is indignant at the maitre d's superciliousness, and refuses to leave when asked. His attempt at leaving a tip is also unsuccessful. The maitre d' then threatens to call the police, to which Ferris replies not to bother; he will be phoning them himself. Clandestinely, however, he calls an internal line within the restaurant instead. The maitre d', thinking that an incoming call is pending, tries to take the receiver from Ferris, but is angrily brushed off. Annoyed, he then heads for another phone further into the building instead. Cameron pleads with Ferris to leave before things become any more complicated, but Ferris is determined to get his own way – as he explains to camera, if he's going to be brought down, it certainly won't be by an arrogant snob like the maitre d'. Sloane takes the receiver from Ferris, and when the maitre d' answers she asks to speak to Abe Froman. The maitre d' asks for Froman's general appearance, so Sloane precisely describes Ferris's current outfit. Smelling a rat, the maitre d' then switches to the other active line, only to hear Cameron impersonating a police sergeant.

We then immediately cut to Ferris, Cameron and Sloane, all comfortably seated at one of the tables in the restaurant as they consult their respective menus. The maitre d' is repentant over the earlier 'misunderstanding', and not even Ferris's barbed comments can pierce the older man's studied contrition. As he leaves, Ferris gently chides Cameron for not having enough faith in his legendary powers of persuasion.

Again we see Ferris managing to get one over on an authority figure with considerable panache. Even when his friends are of the opinion that Ferris is about to run out of luck, he manages to pull an ace from out of his sleeve. It seems, as in the case with his running antipathy with Rooney, that the more despotic and draconian his opponent, the more determined Ferris is to get the upper hand.

Jeanie is standing at the end of a high school corridor, deep in thought. We hear her internal monologue as the camera slowly approaches her. She momentarily considers whether Ferris really is as annoying and exasperating as she has always judged him to be. After all, her parents bought her a car, while he had to put up with a computer instead. Eventually, however, her antipathy wins through as she is needled once again by the agonising realisation that Ferris always manages to get what he aims for without ever getting caught out, while she inevitably comes off second-best.

In the gents' toilet of the restaurant, Ferris is washing his hands as he addresses the camera (via his reflection in the mirror). He discusses the fact that, while his own family is undeniably dysfunctional, the peculiarities of the Buellers are as nothing when compared to those of the Fryes. Intercutting with occasional shots of Cameron looking twitchy and socially ill-at-ease in the restaurant, Ferris laments the unhappy environment that makes up his friend's home, which he blames for Cameron's perpetual belief that he is ill. As Ferris continues to preen himself and comb his hair, he expresses concern for his friend, obviously feeling that Cameron deserves better out of life. Tipping the attendant and stopping to take a complimentary mint on the way out, Ferris has only just left the room when his father emerges from one of the toilet cubicles.

Back in Rooney's office, Jeanie arrives looking to meet with the dean. Grace, still at her desk, explains that Rooney has left the building on personal business, but won't elaborate on when he's due back. Jeanie then refuses to discuss her own business with Grace, and leaves in an even worse mood than when she first turned up. Grace asks her if she shouldn't be in her consumer education class, to which Jeanie responds to the effect that she couldn't care less.

This scene signals for the first time that Jeanie's irritation has reached a level such that she may be considering informing on Ferris's waywardness – a course of action that she has so far considered out of bounds. However, her lack of response to Grace also suggests that she may still be taking into account the full range of her options.

At the main doorway of Chez Quiz, Ferris is alarmed to discover his father at the bottom of the restaurant's steps, deep in conversation with some business associates. Ferris bemoans the odds of such an unfortunate coincidence, although as yet Tom has not noticed their presence. Cameron immediately suggests that they confess their truancy to Tom, but Ferris is absolutely opposed to it, believing that the game is never up. All three don dark glasses and stealthily manage to steal Tom's cab, which is waiting beside him on the street. Before Tom can even notice that the taxi has departed, however, another one has already taken its place.

In a much quieter area, Rooney is parking up, obviously on the lookout for Ferris. Ostentatious music strikes up, reminiscent of an old TV detective show. Getting out of his car, he puts on a pair of dark glasses to disguise his appearance; they are of the flip-up variety, but look comical due to the fact that he isn't wearing any conventional spectacles beneath them. He walks into a busy pizza parlour, bustling with activity, as he casts his eye over the multitude within. Eventually he spots a figure at an arcade machine who is wearing a jacket identical to Ferris's, and heads over for a confrontation. (From the design of the arcade cabinet, the game that is being played is Data East's *Karate Champ* (1984), but the sound effects that are heard throughout the exchange actually sound more like samples from Namco's famous *Pac-Man* (1980).) However, Rooney's threatening tone doesn't go down at all well when the mysterious figure turns around to reveal the face of a young woman, her hairstyle fashionably cropped. Before he has a chance to withdraw his badly-chosen words, the woman spits a mouthful of cola over him with a straw.

Rooney heads over to the eatery's checkout area so that he can dry himself off with a couple of napkins. A baseball game is being played on a television mounted on a nearby wall. As Rooney is temporarily unable to see while he wipes the cola out of his eyes, he completely misses televised footage of Ferris and Cameron celebrating among the spectators at Chicago's Wrigley Field, which shows Ferris catching a wayward baseball that has been hit into the crowd. By the time Rooney's vision is unimpaired, the television camera has moved on to another shot. A nearby cook is rather nonplussed when Rooney, having been told that the game is currently drawn, asks who is winning.

These scenes mark the beginning of Rooney's catastrophic (and, it transpires, hopelessly doomed) quest to bring Ferris down. Hughes brilliantly juxtaposes the image of Ferris and friends donning stylish shades in their previous scene with Rooney wearing his bizarre-looking flip-top sunglasses. But just as Rooney's dignity is punctured by his unexpected case of mistaken identity – and, more to the point, the drenching that follows it – the worst is most certainly still to come.

Out at the baseball park at Wrigley Field, Ferris is still enjoying himself to the full. Even Cameron is finally starting to let his hair down. Momentarily cutting to an exterior shot of the park, a 'Save Ferris' notice is being clearly displayed on a large digital display. (This marks the beginning of a series of running visual gags throughout the film, each contributing high-profile publicity around the Chicago area of Ferris's plight.) Back among the spectators, Sloane looks bored rigid as more of the baseball game is played out, while Ferris jokingly reminds Cameron that if they weren't bunking off, they'd currently be enduring a gym class.

Moving seamlessly to the school's playing fields, a coach is currently driving around on a small motorised vehicle shouting encouragement to a class of breathless students as they jog around a circuit on the grassy sports ground. In the foreground, Jeanie drives up in her car and momentarily comes to a halt. Glancing at Ferris's panting classmates, she mirrors Ferris's own realisation of where he should be if he hadn't managed to pull off his absence, which makes her resent him all the more.

Rooney is pulling up in his car on the street outside the Buellers' house. Striding up to the front door, he rings the doorbell, which we see — thanks to a very quick shot from the house's interior — has set in motion some elaborate electric circuitry. Seconds later, Ferris's voice is piped through an intercom system. He explains that he is unable to come to the door due to his current state of infirmity, but that his parents are both contactable on their business phone numbers. However, Rooney is having none of it. He repeatedly insists that Ferris should come to the door and discuss the nature of his absence with him in greater detail. However, a more detailed shot of Ferris's jury-rigged doorbell system reveals that all of his responses have been recorded onto a cassette tape, and thus Rooney obviously has no chance of a genuine response. Angered at Ferris's apparent refusal to take the matter seriously, Rooney rings the doorbell again, but when he is faced with an exact repeat of the same message he catches on to the fact that he is listening to a recording.

Moving away from the door, Rooney begins to sneak around the house's perimeter, trying to take a look through some of the ground floor windows. The earth nearby is muddy, however, and he has trouble keeping his balance. When attempting to look over some high window shutters, he loses a shoe in a mucky quagmire, and then ends up soaking the legs of his trousers when he accidentally starts water running through a garden hose. Retrieving his shoe, he desperately tries to rinse the mud from it, but only succeeds in drenching himself further in the process.

Rooney's descent into professional (and possibly psychological) oblivion is being firmly established here, for his increasingly desperate attempts to gain evidence of Ferris's truancy from within his family residence is the ultimate source of his downfall. With the seeds of his determination now fully sown, his growing obsession is demanding to be fed.

Back on the outskirts of Chicago, the car park valet and his colleague are racing Mr Frye's Ferrari along an open stretch of road. A quick shot shows that the odometer has already increased, and the speedometer isn't exactly flat-lining either. As John Williams's opening theme from George Lucas's *Star Wars* (1977) plays in the background, the valet and his friend seem ecstatic at the exhilarating experience of speed that the Ferrari is affording them.

On the Buellers' back doorstep, a still-soggy Rooney is tying his shoelaces. He turns, spots what appears to be a large cat-flap in the back door, and decides that he's going to try to force entry to the house. Rooney quickly discovers that he has no chance of gaining access through the flap, which is too small to accommodate his frame, but before he can withdraw he is faced by a ferocious, slobbering guard-dog. The dog has been resting in the kitchen, previously unaware of Rooney's presence. Rooney's bungling attempts to sweet-talk it into submission are entirely in vain, however, and the dog chases him back out into the garden. Switching to a view from one of the houses' windows, we can see Rooney racing back and forward as the snapping dog follows in close pursuit. The sound of tearing linen can be heard.

Ferris, Cameron and Sloane are heading for the Art Institute of Chicago, established in an impressive exterior shot. Moving inside, they can be seen joining in with a tour of elementary schoolkids, before the camera moves on to several close-up shots of various different works of art. The characters also strike a variety of poses in front of numerous pieces, many of their stances being ironic, and Ferris and Sloane take a few moments apart to share a kiss. Cameron, meanwhile, becomes fixated on the image of a happy child standing next to its mother in a painting, Georges Seurat's *Sunday Afternoon on La Grande Jatte*. This again reinforces the notion of the pain he suffered during the course of his own melancholic infancy. But the more that Cameron tries to focus on the child, the less detail he is able to discern.

Next we move to a variety of exterior shots showing a vibrant and well-attended street pageant – the Von Steuben Day Parade. The inner-city traffic is shown as being at a near-standstill due to the passing procession. Cameron thoughtfully tries not to look as Ferris and Sloane kiss, but eventually reminds them both that they will all need to leave soon in order to get the car back safely. Ferris disputes the matter, claiming that they still have a few hours to kill, but Cameron is still anxious, claiming that it will be his neck on the line – not Ferris's – if Mr Frye discovers that the car isn't back in the garage by the time of his return from work. Ferris reproaches his friend, reminding him of all the incredible sights they've witnessed in the city so far, but he soon discovers that his protestations are falling on deaf ears – Cameron has become even more anxious than usual. Looking around for the cause of the disquiet, Ferris discovers to his horror that Tom is sitting in a cab directly adjacent to their own. Before Ferris's father can recognise them, however, Cameron and Ferris duck below window-level, leaving only Sloane visible (and disguised with sunglasses). On the floor of the cab, Ferris and Cameron take turns at feverishly rubbing a lucky rabbit's paw. Looking across from his cab, Tom obviously finds Sloane – who he does not recognise – visually alluring, but does his best to stop staring at her indulgently. Instead, he buries his head in his issue of *The Chicago Sun-Times*. The front cover bears a story about a neighbourhood uniting in support of a certain ailing teenager.

Rooney is watching very cautiously through a hole in the Buellers' garden gate as their dog tears into one of his shoes. He tries – incredibly gingerly – to peer over the top of the gate to get a better view, but the dog immediately races for him, almost managing to jump high enough to bite him. Alarmed, Rooney leaps back to consider his next move.

The parade is still continuing as Cameron and Sloane weave their way through the assembled crowd. They have temporarily lost Ferris, much to Cameron's manifest fretfulness. However, before he can rattle through a full list of potential places he may have gone (most of them solely with the intentional purpose of making Cameron panic), a familiar voice booms out of a nearby speaker, dedicating a song to an individual named Cameron Frye. The pair look up in horror to see Ferris, in his element on the crest of a passing float, flanked by dancers in traditional German dress as he mimes along stylishly to Wayne Newton's 'Danke Schoen' (1963). (A directional sign shown behind the float's accompanying accordionist stipulates that the parade is taking place on Dearborn Street.) This time even Sloane is convinced that Ferris has gone too far. However, before she can protest any further, she and Cameron are rounded up and pushed back into the crowd by a couple of passing policemen. Still at the top of his game, Ferris continues with the song as the parade's apparently-impressed panel of judges look on.

As Cameron and Sloane walk away from the parade area, Cameron bemoans the fact that Ferris always manages to succeed at everything that he sets his mind on, while he finds difficulty in everything, from his miserable home life to facing his fears for the future. His tone is a mixture of admiration and envy. When he mourns the fact that he has no real idea of where he is headed in life, Sloane mentions that he does at least have the certainty of college still to come. But, as Cameron asks, what purpose will be served by his attendance there when nothing really interests him? Sloane replies that nothing much interests her either, and so they do at least have some common ground where that is concerned. Sloane wonders aloud what Ferris will end up doing with his life, to which Cameron speculates wryly that he might become a fry cook.

In this short but pivotal scene, Cameron manages to delineate the core difference between himself and Ferris, even if he can't fully comprehend why this disparity has come to be established. Ferris's success largely comes from his absolute sense of self-belief. Cameron, on the other hand, has virtually no self-esteem whatsoever, which constantly impacts on his worldview and his conception of what he can (and can't) achieve in life. While Ferris appears to be fully cognisant of this distinction, it still seems to be lost on Cameron.

There then follows a short but very entertaining musical interlude, where Ferris – still ensconced atop the parade float – bursts energetically into a mimed rendition of the Beatles's cover of 'Twist and Shout' (1964). He has ample support from a brass band, and his performance is intercut with shots of other Chicago denizens enjoying the music, ranging from a nearby construction worker (complete with hard-hat) to a group of synchronised dancers. Even the judging panel get in on the act. Slightly more surprising is that Tom's office is in one of the buildings overlooking the parade, and we join him as he looks out of the window and can't resist a little boogie in time with the music. Every time Hughes cuts back to Ferris in the float, however, the scene appears a little more lively, and the crowd slightly more densely packed. The assembled multitude burst into rapturous applause as Ferris reaches his triumphant conclusion. He is handed a baton as he waves to the immense audience around him.

Back at the Buellers' house, a delivery man is returning to his van, having dropped something off at the family's front door. We move closer to discover that Rooney has taken possession of the delivery, which is a large potted flower arrangement. He is less than impressed to learn from the attached greetings card that the gift has been sent from the staff and faculty of the school's English department. As the delivery man blows his horn to signal his departure, a livid Rooney gestures obscenely back at him. From the way that Rooney is carrying the arrangement, it is clear that it is actually quite hefty. We then promptly move back to a wide shot of the house's exterior as Rooney advances from the doorway, heading for the gate to the backyard. He whistles and calls for the guard-dog, making clear his intended use for Ferris's floral gift.

Jeanie is parking her car nearby. She gets out to discover –

much to her abhorrence and disbelief – a huge balloon flying high over the rooftops in the vicinity which clearly bears the 'Save Ferris' slogan. Her disgusted expression speaks volumes.

Rooney is peeking victoriously over the Buellers' garden gate, his voice dripping derision as he wishes the guard dog pleasant dreams. We then see a medium close-up of the dog lying unconscious on the paving of the yard, the shattered remnants of the floral arrangement scattered around it. However, from its gentle snoring sounds, we are aware that Rooney has stunned the animal rather than killed it outright.

Here we see Rooney's irrationalism continuing to mount. By effectively staking out Ferris's house, he crosses a line from professional rectitude into the territory of a personal vendetta. But now he has gone one step further, stealing private property and then destroying it in an act of unabashed animal cruelty. Whether – as we are led to suspect – this is an act of revenge for the dog's earlier attack on him, or merely another step along the road to gaining entry to Ferris's house, Rooney is continuing to hurtle down the road to catastrophe.

Jeanie's car is now arriving on the Buellers' driveway. She wastes no time in getting out and heading into the house. Rooney, still unseen at the side of the building, hears her arrival. Inside, Jeanie races upstairs and throws open the door to Ferris's room. The force of the door swinging open is too much for Ferris's jury-rigged mechanism to bear, and the mannequin in his bed sits bolt upright. Her suspicions of Ferris's deception now confirmed beyond doubt, Jeanie is enraged.

Rooney, meanwhile, has crept back to the front door. On discovering that the door is now unlocked, he hesitates momentarily, then decides to quietly gain entry. Upstairs, Jeanie is on the phone to her mother's business line. However, from the tone of her conversation it is clear that her mother is out on business and the intended time of her return is not known. Jeanie, if possible, is growing ever more incensed. Back downstairs, Rooney is starting to creep stealthily through the house. Jeanie hears him gently closing the front door, and – confused – gently sneaks down the stairs to investigate. Her trainers make no noise on the stair carpet. Rooney makes his way into the kitchen, still looking for evidence of Ferris's truancy. This is intercut with a shot of Jeanie's legs and feet, still silent, pacing along the parquet flooring of the hall. Jeanie is convinced that it is Ferris who she hears sneaking back into the house. Rooney, on the other hand, believes Jeanie to be Ferris. Jeanie jumps out of the doorway into the kitchen, expecting to ambush Ferris and catch him in the act. Rooney, on the other hand, is near-simultaneously pouncing out of the kitchen in expectation of apprehending Ferris. Shocked, Jeanie now believes that the house has been invaded by an intruder (which, in effect, is has), but is too scared to recognise Rooney. She attacks him with a number of rapid high-kicks to the head, knocking him out cold. He falls hard onto the kitchen floor as Jeanie, screaming, races back upstairs to the relative safety of her room. Unknown to Rooney as he lies unconscious on the ground, his car (which is parked next to a fire hydrant) is currently being ticketed by a traffic warden on the street outside.

Ferris, Cameron and Sloane are laughing and joking back at the car park. Cameron is still expressing his disbelief at Ferris's audacity in taking such a prominent part in the parade, to which Ferris replies that anyone who really wanted to catch him out would never be attending such a stirring event in the first place. As they talk, the valet arrives with the apparently-undamaged Ferrari. Ferris rebukes Cameron for his earlier lack of faith, though Cameron is still not entirely convinced of the valet's honesty. As the friends get back in the car, Ferris tips the valet again – much to the man's silent amusement. When the Ferrari speeds away into Chicago, the valet and his associate celebrate the fact that they've managed to pull off their impromptu joyride without any adverse consequences.

Cutting back to the street outside the Buellers' house, Rooney's car is now heavily ticketed – there are at least four more official documents tucked under the windscreen wipers alongside the original one. Meanwhile, a frantic Jeanie is in her room and on the phone to the police. It soon becomes apparent from the one side of the conversation we hear that the operator is sceptical of her account – though to her considerable disdain, they do take the time to wish Ferris a speedy recovery. Fuming, Jeanie slams down the receiver.

Back outside, Rooney's car is now being prepared for towing by the authorities. In the Buellers' kitchen, Rooney has regained consciousness and is nursing his wounds with some running water from the sink. Jeanie's voice comes over the house's intercom system and informs the 'intruder' that she has telephoned for police assistance. Rooney turns around in alarm, a ragged piece of paper handkerchief poking comically from one of his bloodied nostrils. Jeanie further elaborates on her earlier statement by adding the fact that she is in possession of her father's gun, and – just to ward off any ideas of intimate attack – is suffering from an appallingly intense infection of herpes. Rooney, growing ever more anxious by the minute, wastes no time in departing. As he does so, a close-up of the kitchen floor reveals that he has accidentally dropped his wallet.

Rooney arrives outside just to see his car being towed away. He shouts out to the driver of the tow-truck, but is ignored. He then races to unlock the driver's side door of his elevated car, but the truck is moving too quickly. Rooney, however, is not quick enough to retrieve his keys in time, and so they are lost along with the car. Now in the throes of mounting hysteria, he screams profanely and gestures frenetically at the driver of the truck, but to no avail. Left with no other obvious choice, he tears after the rapidly-accelerating truck – a task made rather more difficult by the fact that he is still missing one of his shoes, reducing him to an amusing waddle as he tries to run.

Here we see Rooney finally starting to tip over the edge from a state of irrationality into out-and-out mental instability. His comical attempts to rail at the authorities, albeit fruitlessly, are all the more ironic given his own draconian adherence to following the official rules above all else. Yet even now we have not quite seen him reach his lowest ebb.

As the Ferrari cruises though downtown Chicago, Cameron – knowing that they are on the homeward stretch – finally seems to be mildly relaxed. Ferris, however, is anything but – he has just noticed that the odometer is registering almost two hundred more miles than it had when they left Mr Frye's garage. When Cameron notices this, the effect is immediate – an extreme close-up of his mouth, slowly drawing back as we follow his scream outward.

This in turn reveals an expression of total panic, articulating his frame of mind quite efficiently. A rapid montage of shots then follows, depicting a number of different areas of the city as Cameron's anguished shriek continues unabated. Ferris continues to drive while Cameron appears to be hyperventilating, or possibly on the brink of entering some kind of coma. Sloane is becoming increasingly concerned about their friend's wellbeing.

A close-up shot reveals an unfamiliar-looking finger pressing the doorbell at the Buellers' front door. This, in turn, triggers Ferris's recorded message. Upstairs, Jeanie risks a peek from her hiding place under her duvet. Hugely relieved, believing that the police have come to her aid, she races out of her room and down the stairs. However, on hurriedly answering the door, she is rather crestfallen to find herself face-to-face with what appears to be a strip-o-gram dressed as a nurse, complete with a rather creepy-looking entourage. Obviously having been booked with Ferris in mind, the new arrival isn't given a chance to get through her well-rehearsed introductory spiel before Jeanie slams the door in her face.

At a picturesque waterside sight-seeing spot, Cameron is lying out cold on a low wall while Sloane tries to coax some kind of reaction out of him. To camera, Ferris is expressing trepidation about his friend's mental wellbeing. Knowing how uptight Cameron is at the best of times, Ferris is concerned that the prospect of Mr Frye's ire has finally pushed him to snapping point. Ferris also appears worried that his own freewheeling attitude in inviting Cameron to join his day off may have been – at least partly – to blame for the current predicament. As they only have a few months of high school together, following which they will both take summer jobs and then enrol at college (probably in different places), Ferris knows that their friendship – which has lasted since childhood – will probably only survive a little longer before they both go their separate ways in life. This is part of the reason for his absolute determination that they have a good time on his prized day of absence from school. He goes on to consider his relationship with Sloane; as she is a year younger than him, she still has to go through her senior year in high school, and Ferris is unsure how they will be able to keep their romance alive when he is in college.

Cameron still shows no sign of responding to Sloane's repeated attempts to communicate with him. Ferris bemoans the fact that Cameron has never been in love – or, leastways, has never had his love reciprocated. Thus in Ferris's opinion, when Cameron does finally end up striking it lucky with a potential partner, his growing desperation for companionship and affection will almost certainly lead him into a unbalanced relationship with a woman who has no respect for him. Knowing that their time is growing short, Sloane worries that their current approach to coaxing Cameron out of his catatonic state is not working, and suggests that they try something else.

The above scene is interesting, for it is one of the very few in the film where Ferris acknowledges that there are certain forces in life that he can neither outsmart nor manipulate. He knows that he and Cameron are almost certain to drift apart, as may also be the case with Sloane. And yet, rather than grieve over the inevitable, he makes a conscious, life-affirming choice instead to revel in the short time that they have left together, and to make the most of their shared company while he still can.

Ferris and Sloane are luxuriating in a large swimming pool located in Sloane's back garden. Cameron is seated on a plastic folding chair at the end of a diving board, still completely spaced out. Sloane continues with her attempts to talk him out of his strange waking unconsciousness, but is still meeting with no success. Ferris opines that perhaps Cameron really has been pushed into a kind of mental flux by the distressing way that events have transpired. Then, without warning, Cameron falls off his chair and pitches over into the pool. As he remains totally unresponsive in the water, Ferris is alarmed that he may drown, and dives in after him. At the bottom of the pool, however, Cameron is showing an awareness of his surroundings. Ferris grabs his friend and manages to drag him out of danger, with help from Sloane on the surface. He tries desperately to revive Cameron, who remains impassive. Then, suddenly, Cameron smiles and starts joking, proving that he has finally emerged from his catatonic state. Realising that the apparent drowning was a hoax, Ferris is initially angered at having been hoodwinked, but soon sees the funny side and is relieved to have his friend back with him. He pulls Sloane down into the pool with them, and the three start to clown around together.

Jeanie is seated in the waiting area of Shermer Police Station. Officers and staff go quietly about their business around her. A delinquent in a leather jacket is seated next to her, cracking his knuckles. His red-rimmed eyes suggest that he has not had any sleep for some time. He tries to strike up a conversation with Jeanie, though she is reluctant to interact with him. Undeterred, he lets her know that he has been taken in for questioning on drug-related charges, and in turn asks what she's doing there. Jeanie responds that she is not entirely sure of the answer to this question. His further attempts at discussion are initially brushed off, particularly when he (rather surreally) criticises her eye make-up. However, his persistence eventually pays off, and Jeanie explains about her grievance with her brother and the fact that he continually manages to evade suspicion or apprehension despite the outlandish audacity of his schemes. She also clarifies how she got to her current location; after calling the police, officers arrived to discover that there was no intruder in the house (Rooney having left the premises), and as such she was taken back to the station on suspicion of making a hoax call. The delinquent listens carefully to her story, then tells her that in his opinion, her problem does not lie with her brother, but rather with herself. He suggests that she should concentrate on the potential that her own life has, rather than resenting her brother for the success of his conniving plans. Jeanie seems to contemplate this, though she continues to remain otherwise disdainful of the delinquent. He does little to help his case when he suggests that she should talk to a very helpful individual that he knows named Ferris Bueller, who might hold the answer to her problems.

Hughes exercises considerable lightness of touch in the juxtaposition of this scene and the one which follows it. Here, we see Jeanie starting for the first time to question whether her animosity towards Ferris is actually a substitute for dissatisfaction with her own life, thus setting in motion a pronounced change in her character. This is contrasted in the next scene with an even more overwhelming transformation of Cameron's character.

In Mr Frye's garage, the stationary Ferrari is mounted on a couple of metal stands. A small concrete block has been wedged against one of its pedals in order to force it into reverse. This, as Ferris indicated earlier, is a desperate attempt to turn back the figures on the now-greatly-increased odometer. The friends are sitting on a couple of benches outside the garage. Cameron is explaining what went through his mind while he was still in a state of catatonia. He describes a process whereby he started to really observe his behaviour for once, and came to the conclusion that his endless worry and self-loathing over the years had all been pointless and in vain. He makes a conscious choice to change his ways and become a more autonomous individual, better equipped to shape his own destiny. Cameron also says for the first time how much he will miss Ferris and Sloane in the coming year, when they will all be studying in different places. Out of the blue, Sloane asks Cameron if he was watching her getting changed into her swimwear while he was supposedly in the throes of his pseudo-coma. Cameron evades answering this question directly, tactfully deciding to return to the garage to check on the car.

Moments later, Ferris hears an alarmed cry coming from near the Ferrari – Cameron has discovered that their plan isn't working, and the odometer won't go into reverse. Ferris suggests breaking open the odometer and moving the figures backwards by hand, but Cameron decides against it. Instead, Cameron tearfully reaches breaking point and rages against the injustices that have been perpetuated on his life by his father. Furious at years of being bullied and told what he should and shouldn't do, he finally comes to the conclusion that the problem never lay with his dictatorial father, but rather with his own inability to stand up for himself. Pledging that from now on he will take control of his own affairs and determine the future of his life, Cameron channels all of his animosity towards his father into an attack on the car. Fuming, he repeatedly kicks the Ferrari, breaking a headlight and denting the hood and bumper. Sloane moves to stop him in case he regrets it later, but Ferris – sensing the landmark alteration in his friend's psychology – holds her back.

The concerted violence towards the Ferrari appears to have

the required cathartic effect on Cameron, who seems incredibly relieved that he has finally made a stand against his father's tyranny. Ferris and Sloane look on, slightly dazed at the pending consequences of what is going on in front of them. Cameron explains that when his father returns from work, he will finally be forced to deal directly with him. Cameron will no longer have to continually live in terror of Mr Frye's potential loss of temper, as he is choosing to face it candidly. Only then will he receive the closure that he so desperately desires.

Resting his foot triumphantly on the dented hood of the Ferrari, Cameron looks on in shocked amazement as the car – still running in reverse – is knocked off of its metal support struts, and then careens at speed out of one of the garage's large rear windows. (A very skilful reverse angle shot is taken from the Ferrari's point of view, clearly showing the look of awestruck horror on Cameron's face.) The car lands some distance below, lurching through the tightly-packed green trees behind the house. Stunned, Ferris and Sloane rush to the broken window to survey the extent of the damage. Sloane offers a momentary enigmatic smile, living in the moment and demonstrating an appreciation for the unexpected. Cameron, who still can't quite believe what has happened, desperately questions what he has done. Ferris responds to his question by answering that the Ferrari has met its demise. Dreading every step, Cameron moves to join his friends at the window, peering down to be met with the sight of the car's wreckage smouldering on the ground. It is partially covered by branches, and almost certainly damaged beyond repair. A close-up shot reveals that the car has only been stopped by the presence of a wire-mesh fence at the boundary of the garden.

Cameron is momentarily too shaken to talk. He absently kicks a small piece of broken glass from the frame of the window over into the garden below, still coming to terms with what has happened. None of the three can quite believe what they've just seen. Moving back into the main body of the garage, Cameron is still obviously disturbed. Ferris offers to take the blame for what has happened, based on the fact that Mr Frye already holds him in contempt. He also tells Cameron that he considers himself responsible for the way things transpired, given that it was he who insisted on taking the Ferrari out of the garage that morning. But Cameron has made up his mind. Telling Ferris that he wouldn't have let him drive the Ferrari that day unless he was willing to face the potential consequences, he will face up to his father on his return and have a long-overdue conversation with him. As the scene ends, a lingering close-up of Cameron's face shows the determination and new-found resolve in his expression.

Cameron's emotional journey is at the very core of the narrative of *Ferris Bueller's Day Off*, and these scenes form its triumphant climax. With his new sense of purpose, Cameron has at last put himself in command of his own free will, and we know without doubt that by crossing a crucially important line – the destruction of his father's one true pride and joy – he will force the very confrontation that he has spent his life dreading and trying to avoid. He has now come full-circle from the fearful neurotic of the film's first act, and is ready to face not only his belligerent father Morris, but also his future.

Back at the police station, Katie is speaking to a detective in his office about the situation that has unfolded during the day with Jeanie. Katie expresses incredulity that Jeanie would be out of school without authorisation, much less that she would make a hoax call to the police. The detective responds that for whatever reason Jeanie made the call, she was obviously genuinely frightened. Katie assures him that she and Tom will later be discussing the matter with her in detail. As she heads out of his office, the detective asks Katie to pass on the best wishes of everyone at the station to Ferris, who he hopes will soon make a full recovery. Katie seems mildly nonplussed by this.

In the waiting area, Jeanie is enjoying a passionate (and surprising) clinch with the delinquent. An annoyed Katie clears her throat to break up their embrace, then tells Jeanie that she wants her out of the police station as quickly as possible. As Katie heads off, Jeanie – her general disposition now much more light-hearted than before – says her goodbyes to the delinquent (who asks her name, but when she replies never offers his own). As Jeanie leaves, she finds herself almost dizzy with elation, though Katie – shouting from the ground floor – is less than impressed by what has transpired.

Outside Sloane's house, she and Ferris are making their own goodbyes for the day. Sloane tells him how much she has enjoyed herself, and asks if he's sure that Cameron will be alright given the tumultuous events that took place earlier. Ferris replies that he feels certain that Cameron will be absolutely fine, and quite possibly for the first time ever. Sloane and Ferris look at each other longingly. Smiling, Sloane then asks Ferris if he knew precisely what he was planning from the minute the day started. Ferris won't elaborate though, and kisses her instead. They are reluctant to part their embrace, but Ferris discovers that the time is five minutes to six – his family will be due back at the house at any time. Pausing only to give her a peck on the cheek – and the assurance that he'll call her later – Ferris races off towards his home. As he leaves, Sloane calls out to Ferris to tell him that she loves him, to which Ferris responds that he reciprocates fully. Smiling, Sloane assures herself aloud that one day the two of them be married.

This scene underscores the depth of affection that exists between Ferris and Sloane, which is hinted at throughout the film. Her consent to the proposal of marriage that he made earlier, though Ferris does not hear it, perhaps undermines his earlier regrets that the two of them are liable to drift apart over the course of the coming year.

Ferris is fighting his way through a patch of greenery between houses as Jeanie's car heads along a nearby road. In the car, Katie is complaining bitterly about Jeanie's conduct, particularly as she ended up losing a deal at work due to her having to pick Jeanie up from the police station. This is intercut with a shot of Ferris, still racing home on foot, and then quickly returns to Jeanie driving along the road. Unexpectedly, Ferris sprints out of the undergrowth right into the path of Jeanie's car, causing her to make an emergency stop. Ferris is caught right in front of the hood of Jeanie's car, his identity unmistakeable. However, the car's sudden halt has caused Katie's papers to fly up into the air, obscuring her vision. With a tight close-up of Jeanie's eyes, we can see that she is throwing down the gauntlet to Ferris. As he matches her indignant expression and continues his rush towards home, Jeanie hits the accelerator in order to race him to their mutual destination. Katie is totally oblivious to this situation, her papers once again taking to the air (much to her frustration).

As Jeanie continues to pick up speed, Ferris dives through a hedgerow and races through a series of back gardens. The respective householders, some enjoying dinner, watch in surprise as he tears across their property. We cut between Ferris's progress and Jeanie's high-velocity car. Katie is growing more and more agitated at the apparently purposeless acceleration, while Jeanie becomes increasingly hysterical in response. Her progress soon looks to be curtailed by the arrival of a police patrol car. The officer tries to pull her over for speeding. Jeanie, however, appears to be in no mood to slow down.

Still running, Ferris helps himself to a can of cola from an oblivious barbecue enthusiast as he maintains his trajectory towards the Buellers' house. He only stops momentarily to introduce himself to a couple of beautiful sunbathers as he passes through their garden. Tom, meanwhile, is also making his way home from work in his car. He stops momentarily to find a breath mint from his glove compartment. In so doing, he completely misses seeing Jeanie's car speeding past him, followed by an equally swift patrol car.

Further along the road, Jeanie eventually relents and pulls over to be ticketed. Tom, meanwhile, finds his progress impeded by an elderly driver in front of him who is steering slowly and erratically due to the fact that they are too short to see over the dashboard. Ferris is still jogging through the neighbourhood, and is very nearly caught out by Tom – whose car he accidentally ends up running next to – when Tom overtakes the car that has so far been slowing him down. By sheer fluke, Tom looks away at just the right moment and thus does not recognise Ferris as he desperately cuts away behind the car.

Now increasingly frantic, Ferris takes a short-cut straight through someone's house, heads through another garden, climbs over some children's play equipment, and then takes a jump over a high hedge to land in his own backyard. His arrival is simultaneous with the appearance – at the front of the house – of Jeanie, Katie and (seconds later) Tom.

Jeanie tears through the front door while Ferris, at the rear of the house, finds that the back door is locked. Meanwhile, Katie accosts Tom on the house's front entranceway and explains what has happened with Jeanie, describing her trip to the police station. As the discussion of Jeanie's behaviour continues, the deadpan Tom comes to the opinion that a gunshot could improve the situation.

At the back door, Ferris is desperately scrambling about under the doormat in search of a spare house key. A tattered shoe and trouser leg stamp down next to him, and the camera pans up to reveal — much to Ferris's horror — Ed Rooney. (He now appears to have somehow retrieved his missing shoe from the Buellers' guard-dog.) Holding the door key in question, the supremely battered Rooney informs Ferris (with no small amount of jubilation) that he has caught him red-handed at last. This is briefly intercut with Katie and Tom on the front doorstep deciding to go into the house and check on Ferris's wellbeing. Rooney, meanwhile, is absolutely relishing his moment of victory, explaining to Ferris just how long he's waited for this occasion.

There is some interesting symmetry at play in this scene. In an earlier scene, where Ferris telephones Rooney in his office, Rooney is too shocked to speak. Here, as Rooney rants exultantly in the belief that Ferris has finally being called to account for his truancy, the tables are turned and Ferris is the one who finds himself unable to respond. Therefore, although the two engage in direct interaction only rarely throughout the course of the film, in either instance only one speaks while the other listens. (This, of course, is also true of the one-way conversation Rooney has with the recording on the house intercom.) By using this method, Hughes makes the dry observation that the two characters — polar opposites in terms of personality — quite literally have nothing to say to each other.

We then cut to Jeanie, in the kitchen, listening to the exchange between Rooney and Ferris with a look of immense satisfaction on her face. Tom and Katie are moving into the house's main hallway, which is festooned with many different floral bouquets that have obviously been gifted to Ferris throughout the day. Returning to the back door, Jeanie is peering out of the curtains hanging over a small window to witness Rooney, still savouring the moment, telling Ferris to prepare for another full year of high school – this time, under his own direct tutelage. Before the horrified Ferris has a chance to respond, Jeanie abruptly opens the back door and tells him how worried the family have been about him; they expected him back a while ago. Ferris is stunned at this unexpected turnaround in fortune, particularly as it comes from the hand of his oldest adversary (his amazed glance to camera says it all). She also thanks an equally-confused Rooney for driving Ferris home – how, she asks, could such an infirm person expect to get back from hospital on foot? As Ferris heads rapidly into the house before his luck changes, Rooney affects a totally crushed expression as he realises that defeat has been snatched from the jaws of victory. Before he has time to question Jeanie, however, she informs him that she's found his wallet on the kitchen floor, thus proving that he was the intruder from earlier. Rooney's eyes boggle at this revelation as Jeanie tosses the wallet far into the backyard (and, judging from the watery sound that it makes on impact, straight into a garden pond). She then slams the door, which awakens the until-recently unconscious guard-dog. Rooney looks round with disconsolate inevitability as the dog recognises him and begins to snarl. Jeanie stands elatedly, her back to the door, as the deafening sound of Rooney being attacked by the dog once again can be heard from behind her.

Here we witness that Jeanie, like Cameron, has performed a complete one hundred and eighty degree turn as a character. From an initial determination to prove Ferris's dishonesty at any cost, her epiphany at the police station has gifted her enlightenment enough to not only consider her own objectives as the epicentre of her purpose of being, but has actually led her to embrace this philosophy so fully that she can find it in herself to save Ferris from Rooney's clutches – especially significant when she herself seemed ready to inform on Ferris to Rooney earlier in the day.

Safely returning to his bedroom, Ferris rapidly gets undressed and back into his bed. He realises at the last minute that he has left his hi-fi system on, which is still playing a looped sample of his snoring. He has no time to get out of bed before his parents arrive, but suddenly remembers the baseball that he caught at Wrigley Field earlier in the day. Throwing it across the room, he has the good fortune to hit the hi-fi's standby button, silencing the stereo's speakers. He is doubly relieved that the ball miraculously manages to land in a discarded baseball glove lying on the floor (thus making it look totally innocuous), and all literally seconds before his parents arrive.

Katie comes to Ferris's bedside and gently 'wakes' her son. Ferris, who has been feigning sleep with total conviction, assures them when asked that he is feeling much better, but pleads with them not to allow him any further time off school – his studies are important to him, he explains, and he doesn't want to put his future in jeopardy. Tom assures him that the most important thing is his health; he shouldn't rush to get better and inadvertently make himself feel worse. Ferris grudgingly allows that maybe his father knows best. Katie asks him how he ever managed to become so lovable, to which Ferris answers – with more honesty than they realise – that he could only achieve it through years of careful preparation. Still turning on the charm, he invites his mother to pull up his blanket. She assures him that she'll soon return with some hot soup, before leaving with Tom and closing the door quietly behind them.

Ferris, relieved beyond measure that everything has somehow managed to work out, turns directly to camera and reiterates his earlier point that life moves so quickly, it's important to take the time to slow down every so often in order to fully appreciate it. He smiles devilishly as the scene fades out.

It is interesting to note that these closing events mirror the film's opening scenes, with Ferris's dexterous melange of emotional manipulation, precise calculation and blind luck winning the day just as it had back when he was endeavouring to secure the day off in the first place. He also reinforces the film's central theme – the need to enjoy and recognise the value of life rather than simply be swept along by it. It is this realisation that so profoundly transforms the lives of both Cameron and Jeanie, and – to a lesser extent – gives Sloane the determination that she will not willingly let her relationship with Ferris fail. (It is also pleasing to note the Simple Minds poster next to Ferris's bedroom door, which is publicising 'Don't You Forget About Me', the distinctive title song from *The Breakfast Club*.)

As the end credits roll, a bruised and blooded Rooney is gingerly making his way along the street. A reprise of Yello's 'Oh Yeah' begins to play. Rooney is furiously muttering to himself about the injustice of Ferris managing to evade the reach of his authority at the very last minute. As the camera pans up, we realise that Rooney and his suit seem even more dishevelled than they were previously, and his movements are very stiff and painful-looking. Yet just as Rooney must feel that his indignity can increase no further, a school bus packed full of students draws alongside him. The bus driver recognises him, and seems concerned for his wellbeing. Rooney, now humiliated in front of the students (to say nothing of the impotent rage that he's already experiencing), gives no response. However, when the bus driver offers him a lift, he appears so defeated that he silently acquiesces. The bus comes to a halt in order to let him on. Pausing to straighten his tie, Rooney boards the bus only to discover that he is too tall to stand upright in it. He has to stoop in order to avoid hitting his head against the roof. Glowering, he makes his way past rows and rows of students, their expressions bordering on the incredulous. Eventually, he discovers an empty seat near the back of the bus, next to a geeky-looking girl with an unusually conservative taste in fashion. They regard each other in silence. The student tries to engage him in polite conversation, but the shattered Rooney is having none of it. She then offers him a gum sweet, which he takes and then promptly throws further into the bus. The other students don't seem to know where to look, and appear particularly apprehensive when Rooney notices some obscene graffiti about himself scribbled inside the bus. However, the final ignominy comes when he spots one of their folders, which is embellished with a colourful 'Save Ferris' design. Now clearly feeling that his mortification has reached its lowest ebb, Rooney looks straight to camera, a broken man. Seconds later, the bus pulls away from the kerb, heading off into the distance.

If Cameron's story is at the emotional heart of the film's narrative, then Rooney's descent into injury and humiliation forms its counterpoint. Whereas the other main characters discover life-affirming truths about themselves, or – through their self-belief – show appreciation for the importance and worth of life, Rooney's grudge against Ferris instead leads him to spiral into embarrassment and perhaps even a subtle form of borderline psychosis. Growing more and more out of his depth the further he strays from his 'comfort zone' of his high school, Rooney symbolises everything that is hidebound and unimaginative about bureaucratic authoritarianism, and when he makes the decision to turn his suspicions about Ferris into a deeply personal vendetta, he is totally unprepared for the deleterious effect that this will have on him. By the end of the film, his personal and professional reputation are almost as battered as his physical form, and yet from the school bus sequence we are left in no doubt that his ill-fated experiences have done little if anything to actually change his outlook. Thus while Cameron and Jeanie have both been deeply altered, seeking to confront and overcome their personal demons, the most reductive, damaging factor that faces Ed Rooney is in fact revealed to be his own narrow-minded attitude towards life.

After the end credits have rolled, Ferris – back in his bathrobe – heads down the hallway of his home and expresses surprise that anyone is still watching. He assures the audience that the action has now concluded, and urges them to leave and go back to their business – in effect, underscoring one last time the film's central themes of self-determination and making the most of your life for as long as you can.

FILMOGRAPHY

FERRIS BUELLER'S DAY OFF (1986)

Production Company: Paramount Productions.
Distributor: Paramount Productions.
Director: John Hughes.
Producers: John Hughes and Tom Jacobson.
Associate Producer: Jane Vickerilla.
Executive Producer: Michael Cinich.
Screenplay: John Hughes.
Film Editor: Paul Hirsch.
Cinematography: Tak Fujimoto.
Unit Production Manager: Arne Schmidt.
Original Music: Ira Newborn, Arthur Baker and John Robie.
Production Design: John W. Corso.
Casting: Janet Hirshenson and Jane Jenkins.
Set Decoration: Jennifer Polito.
Costume Design: Marilyn Vance.
Running Time: 103 minutes.

***Main Cast*:**

Matthew Broderick (Ferris Bueller),
Alan Ruck (Cameron Frye),
Mia Sara (Sloane Peterson),
Jeffrey Jones (Ed Rooney),
Jennifer Grey (Jeanie Bueller),
Cindy Pickett (Katie Bueller),
Lyman Ward (Tom Bueller),
Edie McClurg (Grace),
Charlie Sheen (Boy in Police Station),
Ben Stein (Economics Teacher),
Del Close (English Teacher),
Virginia Capers (Florence Sparrow),
Richard Edson (Garage Attendant),
Larry Flash Jenkins (Attendant's Co-Pilot),
Kristy Swanson (Simone Adamley),
Lisa Bellard (Economics Student),
Max Perlich (Anderson),
T. Scott Coffee (Adams),
Jonathan Schmock (Chez Quis Maitre D'),
Joey Viera (Pizza Man).

THEATRICAL RELEASE DATES

Below are the dates that Ferris Bueller's Day Off *made its cinematic debut in various countries around the world.*

Argentina	Thursday 23 October 1986
Australia	Thursday 21 August 1986
France	Wednesday 17 December 1986
Hong Kong	Thursday 8 January 1987
Italy	Thursday 4 December 1986
Japan	Saturday 28 February 1987
Netherlands	Thursday 18 December 1986
Spain	Friday 24 April 1987
UK	Friday 20 February 1987
USA	Wednesday 11 June 1986
West Germany	Thursday 18 December 1986

RELEASE INFORMATION

Due to its popularity with audiences, Ferris Bueller's Day Off has been released many times on DVD and, more recently, it has been issued on Blu-Ray Disc. Listed below are details of some of the more popular versions which are currently available to buy. The film has also been included in many different compilation editions, where it is bundled with other similarly-themed films (mostly originating from the eighties).

UNITED STATES

***Ferris Bueller's Day Off* (Blu-Ray Edition)**
Paramount Home Entertainment
Released 5 May 2009
ASIN: B001S86J1C. UPC: 097361429243

***Ferris Bueller's Day Off* (I Love the 80s DVD Edition)**
Paramount Home Entertainment
Released 5 August 2008
ASIN: B0019GO58W. UPC: 097361379548

***Ferris Bueller's Day Off* ('Bueller... Bueller...' DVD Edition)**
Paramount Home Entertainment
Released 10 January 2006

ASIN: B000BNX4MC. UPC: 097360313345

Ferris Bueller's Day Off (DVD Edition with John Hughes Commentary)
Paramount Home Entertainment
Released 19 October 1999
ASIN: B00001MXXH. UPC: 097360189049

UNITED KINGDOM

Ferris Bueller's Day Off (Blu-Ray Edition)
Paramount Home Entertainment
Released 1 February 2010
ASIN: B002MVPPMI

Ferris Bueller's Day Off ('Bueller... Bueller...' DVD Edition)
Paramount Home Entertainment
Released 29 May 2006
ASIN: B000ERVG6G

Ferris Bueller's Day Off (DVD Edition with John Hughes Commentary)
Paramount Home Entertainment
Released 31 July 2000
ASIN: B00004U40K

THE FILMS OF JOHN HUGHES: A TIMELINE

---

1. *National Lampoon's Class Reunion* (1982)
Dir. Michael Miller
(as screenwriter)

2. *Mr Mom* (1982)
Dir. Stan Dragoti
(as screenwriter)

3. *National Lampoon's Vacation* (1983)
Dir. Harold Ramis
(as screenwriter)

4. *Nate and Hayes* (1983)
Dir. Ferdinand Fairfax
(as screenwriter)

5. *Sixteen Candles* (1984)
Dir. John Hughes
(as director and screenwriter)

6. *The Breakfast Club* (1985)
Dir. John Hughes
(as producer, director and screenwriter)

7. *National Lampoon's European Vacation* (1985)
Dir. Amy Heckerling
(as screenwriter)

8. *Weird Science* (1985)
Dir. John Hughes
(as director and screenwriter)

9. *Pretty in Pink* (1986)
Dir. Howard Deutch
(as executive producer and screenwriter)

10. *Ferris Bueller's Day Off* (1986)
Dir. John Hughes
(as producer, director and screenwriter)

11. *Some Kind of Wonderful* (1987)
Dir. Howard Deutch
(as producer and screenwriter)

12. *Planes, Trains and Automobiles* (1987)
Dir. John Hughes
(as producer, director and screenwriter)

13. *She's Having a Baby* (1988)
Dir. John Hughes
(as producer, director and screenwriter)

14. *The Great Outdoors* (1988)
Dir. Howard Deutch
(as executive producer and screenwriter)

15. *Uncle Buck* (1989)
Dir. John Hughes
(as producer, director and screenwriter)

16. *National Lampoon's Christmas Vacation* (1989)

Dir. Jeremiah S. Chechik
(as producer and screenwriter)

17. *Home Alone* (1990)
Dir. Chris Columbus
(as producer and screenwriter)

18. *Career Opportunities* (1991)
Dir. Bryan Gordon
(as producer and screenwriter)

19. *Only the Lonely* (1991)
Dir. Chris Columbus
(as producer)

20. *Dutch* (1991)
Dir. Peter Faiman
(as producer and screenwriter)

21. *Curly Sue* (1991)
Dir. John Hughes
(as producer, director and screenwriter)

22. *Beethoven* (1992)
Dir. Brian Levant
(as screenwriter, writing as Edmond Dantès)

23. *Home Alone 2: Lost in New York* (1992)
Dir. Chris Columbus
(as producer and screenwriter)

24. *Dennis the Menace* (1993)
Dir. Nick Castle
(as producer and screenwriter)

25. *Baby's Day Out* (1994)
Dir. Patrick Read Johnson
(as producer and screenwriter)

26. *Miracle on 34th Street* (1994)
Dir. Les Mayfield
(as producer and screenwriter)

27. *101 Dalmatians* (1996)
Dir. Stephen Herek
(as producer and screenwriter)

28. *Flubber* (1997)
Dir. Les Mayfield
(as producer and screenwriter)

29. *Home Alone 3* (1997)
Dir. Raja Gosnell
(as producer and screenwriter)

30. *Reach the Rock* (1998)
Dir. William Ryan
(as producer and screenwriter)

31. *Les Visiteurs en Amérique/ Just Visiting* (2001)
Dir. Jean-Marie Poiré
(as screenwriter)

32. *New Port South* (2001)
Dir. Kyle Cooper
(as executive producer)

33. *Maid in Manhattan* (2002)
Dir. Wayne Wang
(story, writing as Edmond Dantès)

34. *Drillbit Taylor* (2008)
Dir. Steven Brill
(story, writing as Edmond Dantès)

FURTHER READING

Austin, Joe, and Michael Nevin Willard, eds, *Generations of Youth: Youth Cultures and History in Twentieth-Century America* (New York: NYU Press, 1998).

Batchelor, Bob, and Scott Stoddart, *The 1980s* (Westport: Greenwood Publishing Group, 2006).

Base, Ron, and David Haslam, *The Movies of the Eighties* (London: Portland, 1990).

Bernstein, Jonathan, *Pretty in Pink: The Golden Age of Teenage Movies* (New York: St. Martin's Press, 1997).

Christie, Thomas A., *John Hughes and Eighties Cinema: Teenage Hopes and American Dreams* (Maidstone: Crescent Moon Publishing, 2009).

Clarke, Jaime, ed., *Don't You Forget About Me: Contemporary Writers on the Films of John Hughes* (New York: Simon Spotlight, 2007).

Gora, Susannah, *You Couldn't Ignore Me If You Tried: The Brat Pack, John Hughes, and Their Impact on a Generation* (New York: Crown Publishing Group, 2010).

Lewis, Jon, *The Road to Romance & Ruin: Teen Films and Youth Culture* (London: Routledge, 1992).

Mallan, Kerry, and Sharyn Pearce, *Youth Cultures: Texts, Images, and Identities* (Westport: Greenwood Publishing Group, 2003).

Mansour, David, *From Abba to Zoom: A Pop Culture Encyclopedia of the Late 20th Century* (Riverside: Andrews McMeel Publishing, 2005).

Müller, Jürgen, *Movies of the 80s* (Köln: Taschen Books, 2002).

Palmer, William J., *The Films of the Eighties: A Social History* (Carbondale: Southern Illinois University Press, 1993).

Prince, Stephen, *A New Pot of Gold: Hollywood Under the Electronic Rainbow, 1980-1989* (Berkeley: University of California Press, 2002).

Prince, Stephen, ed., *American Cinema of the 1980s: Themes and Variations* (Chapel Hill: Rutgers University Press, 2007).

Quart, Alissa, *Branded: The Buying and Selling of Teenagers* (Jackson: Basic Books, 2004).

Rettenmund, Matthew, *Totally Awesome 80s* (New York: Saint Martin's Press, 1996).

Shary, Timothy, *Generation Multiplex: The Image of Youth in Contemporary American Cinema* (Austin: University of Texas Press, 2002).

Shary, Timothy, *Teen Movies: American Youth on Screen* (London: Wallflower Press, 2005).

Tropiano, Stephen, *Rebels and Chicks: A History of the Hollywood Teen Movie* (New York: Back Stage Books, 2006).

ILLUSTRATIONS

Images from *Ferris Bueller's Day Off*.

Some locations: the Art Institute, and Chicago from the Sears Tower.

And some of John Hughes's other movies.

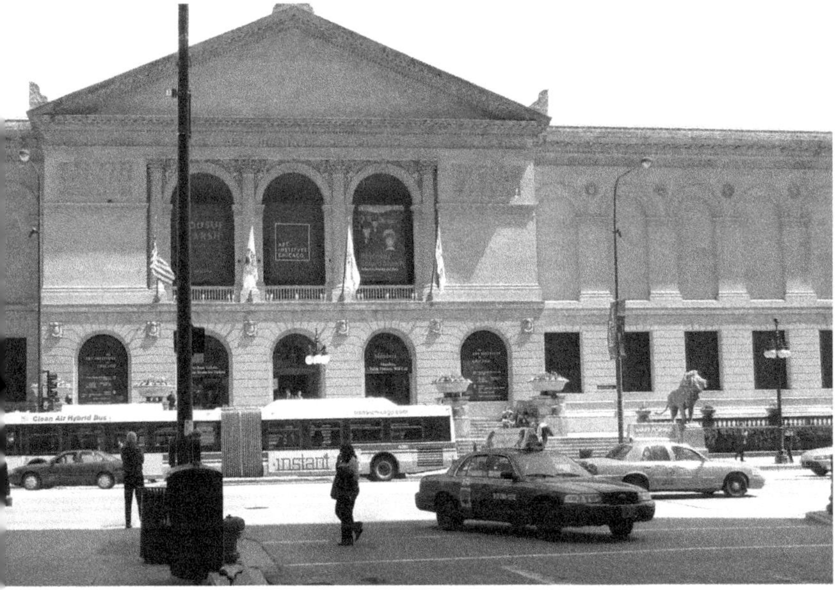
Clean Air Hybrid Bus

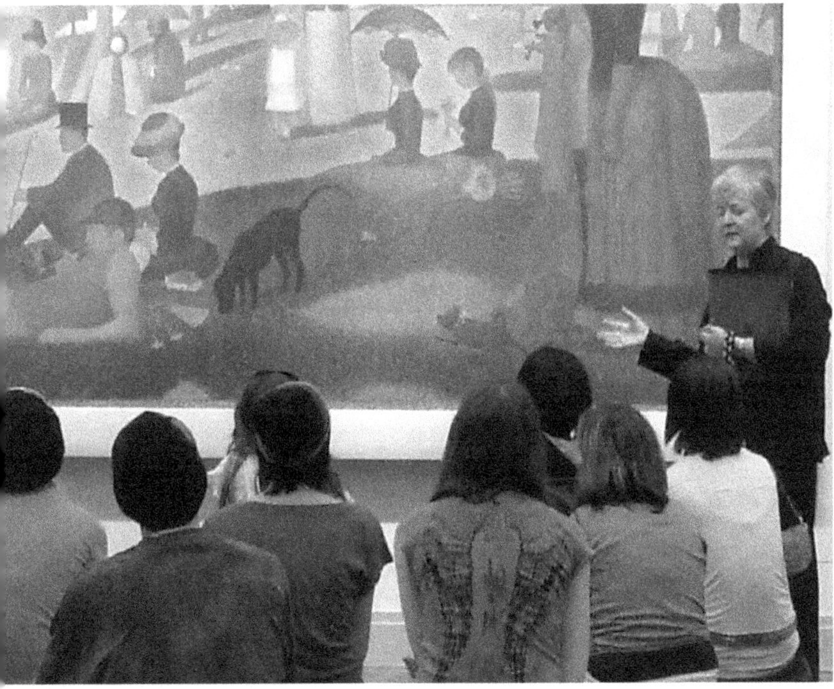

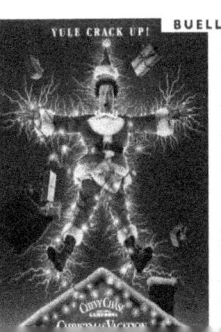

ARTS, PAINTING, SCULPTURE

The Art of Andy Goldsworthy: Complete Works
Andy Goldsworthy: Touching Nature
Andy Goldsworthy in Close-Up
Andy Goldsworthy: Pocket Guide
Andy Goldsworthy In America
Land Art: A Complete Guide
Richard Long: The Art of Walking
The Art of Richard Long: Complete Works
Richard Long in Close-Up
Richard Long: Pocket Guide

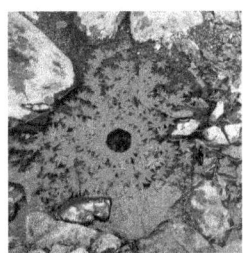

Land Art In the UK
Land Art in Close-Up
Land Art In the U.S.A.
Land Art: Pocket Guide
Installation Art in Close-Up

Minimal Art and Artists In the 1960s and After
Colourfield Painting
Land Art DVD, TV documentary
Andy Goldsworthy DVD, TV documentary
The Erotic Object: Sexuality in Sculpture From Prehistory to the Present Day
Sex in Art: Pornography and Pleasure in Painting and Sculpture
Postwar Art
Sacred Gardens: The Garden in Myth, Religion and Art
Glorification: Religious Abstraction in Renaissance and 20th Century Art
Early Netherlandish Painting
Leonardo da Vinci
Piero della Francesca
Giovanni Bellini
Fra Angelico: Art and Religion in the Renaissance
Mark Rothko: The Art of Transcendence
Frank Stella: American Abstract Artist
Jasper Johns
Brice Marden

Alison Wilding: The Embrace of Sculpture
Vincent van Gogh: Visionary Landscapes
Eric Gill: Nuptials of God
Constantin Brancusi: Sculpting the Essence of Things
Max Beckmann
Gustave Moreau
Caravaggio

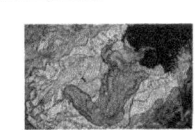

Egon Schiele: Sex and Death In Purple Stockings
Delizioso Fotografico Fervore: Works In Process 1
Sacro Cuore: Works In Process 2
The Light Eternal: J.M.W. Turner
The Madonna Glorified: Karen Arthurs

LITERATURE

J.R.R. Tolkien: The Books, The Films, The Whole Cultural Phenomenon
J.R.R. Tolkien: Pocket Guide
Beauties, Beasts and Enchantment: Classic French Fairy Tales
Tolkien's Heroic Quest
Sexing Hardy: Thomas Hardy and Feminism
Thomas Hardy's *Tess of the d'Urbervilles*
Thomas Hardy's *Jude the Obscure*
Thomas Hardy: The Tragic Novels
Love and Tragedy: Thomas Hardy
The Poetry of Landscape in Hardy
Wessex Revisited: Thomas Hardy and John Cowper Powys
Wolfgang Iser: Essays and Interviews
Petrarch, Dante and the Troubadours
Maurice Sendak and the Art of Children's Book Illustration
Andrea Dworkin

Cixous, Irigaray, Kristeva: The *Jouissance* of French Feminism
Julia Kristeva: Art, Love, Melancholy, Philosophy, Semiotics and Psychoanalysis
Hélene Cixous I Love You: The *Jouissance* of Writing
Luce Irigaray: Lips, Kissing, and the Politics of Sexual Difference
Peter Redgrove: Here Comes the Flood
Peter Redgrove: Sex-Magic-Poetry-Cornwall
Lawrence Durrell: Between Love and Death, East and West
Love, Culture & Poetry: Lawrence Durrell
Cavafy: Anatomy of a Soul

German Romantic Poetry: Goethe, Novalis, Heine, Hölderlin
Novalis: *Hymns To the Night*
Feminism and Shakespeare
Shakespeare: *The Sonnets*
Shakespeare: Love, Poetry & Magic
The Passion of D.H. Lawrence
D.H. Lawrence: Symbolic Landscapes
D.H. Lawrence: Infinite Sensual Violence
Rimbaud: Arthur Rimbaud and the Magic of Poetry
The Ecstasies of John Cowper Powys

Sensualism and Mythology: The Wessex Novels of John Cowper Powys
Amorous Life: John Cowper Powys and the Manifestation of Affectivity (H.W. Fav
Postmodern Powys: New Essays on John Cowper Powys (Joe Boulter)
Rethinking Powys: Critical Essays on John Cowper Powys
Paul Bowles & Bernardo Bertolucci
Rainer Maria Rilke
Joseph Conrad: *Heart of Darkness*
In the Dim Void: Samuel Beckett
Samuel Beckett Goes into the Silence
André Gide: Fiction and Fervour

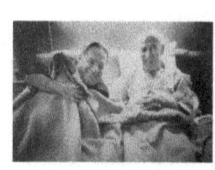

Jackie Collins and the Blockbuster Novel
Blinded By Her Light: The Love-Poetry of Robert Graves
The Passion of Colours: Travels In Mediterranean Lands
Poetic Forms

POETRY

Ursula Le Guin: *Walking In Cornwall*
Peter Redgrove: Here Comes The Flood
Peter Redgrove: Sex-Magic-Poetry-Cornwall
Dante: Selections From the *Vita Nuova*
Petrarch, Dante and the Troubadours
William Shakespeare: *The Sonnets*
William Shakespeare: Complete Poems
Blinded By Her Light: The Love-Poetry of Robert Graves
Emily Dickinson: Selected Poems
Emily Brontë: Poems
Thomas Hardy: Selected Poems
Percy Bysshe Shelley: Poems
John Keats: Selected Poems
D.H. Lawrence: Selected Poems
Edmund Spenser: Poems
Edmund Spenser: *Amoretti*
John Donne: Poems
Henry Vaughan: Poems
Sir Thomas Wyatt: Poems
Robert Herrick: Selected Poems
Rilke: Space, Essence and Angels in the Poetry of Rainer Maria Rilke
Rainer Maria Rilke: Selected Poems
Friedrich Hölderlin: Selected Poems
Arseny Tarkovsky: Selected Poems
Paul Verlaine: Selected Poems
Novalis: *Hymns To the Night*
Arthur Rimbaud: Selected Poems
Arthur Rimbaud: *A Season in Hell*
Arthur Rimbaud and the Magic of Poetry
D.J. Enright: By-Blows
Jeremy Reed: *Brigitte's Blue Heart*
Jeremy Reed: *Claudia Schiffer's Red Shoes*
Gorgeous Little Orpheus
Radiance: New Poems
Crescent Moon Book of Nature Poetry
Crescent Moon Book of Love Poetry
Crescent Moon Book of Mystical Poetry
Crescent Moon Book of Elizabethan Love Poetry
Crescent Moon Book of Metaphysical Poetry
Crescent Moon Book of Romantic Poetry
Pagan America: New American Poetry

MEDIA, CINEMA, FEMINISM and CULTURAL STUDIES

J.R.R. Tolkien: The Books, The Films, The Whole Cultural Phenomenon
J.R.R. Tolkien: Pocket Guide
The *Lord of the Rings* Movies: Pocket Guide
The Ghost Dance: The Origins of Religion
Cixous, Irigaray, Kristeva: The *Jouissance* of French Feminism
Julia Kristeva: Art, Love, Melancholy, Philosophy, Semiotics and Psychoanalysis
Luce Irigaray: Lips, Kissing, and the Politics of Sexual Difference
Hélene Cixous I Love You: The *Jouissance* of Writing
Andrea Dworkin
'Cosmo Woman': The World of Women's Magazines
Women in Pop Music
Discovering the Goddess (Geoffrey Ashe)
The Poetry of Cinema
The Sacred Cinema of Andrei Tarkovsky
Andrei Tarkovsky: Pocket Guide
Andrei Tarkovsky: *Mirror*: Pocket Movie Guide
Andrei Tarkovsky: *The Sacrifice*: Pocket Movie Guide
Walerian Borowczyk: Cinema of Erotic Dreams
Jean-Luc Godard: The Passion of Cinema
Jean-Luc Godard: Pocket Guide
John Hughes and Eighties Cinema
Ferris Buller's Day Off: Pocket Movie Guide
The Cinema of Richard Linklater
Liv Tyler: Star In Ascendance
Blade Runner and the Films of Philip K. Dick
Paul Bowles and Bernardo Bertolucci
Media Hell: Radio, TV and the Press
An Open Letter to the BBC
Detonation Britain: Nuclear War in the UK
Feminism and Shakespeare
Wild Zones: Pornography, Art and Feminism
Sex in Art: Pornography and Pleasure in Painting and Sculpture
Sexing Hardy: Thomas Hardy and Feminism

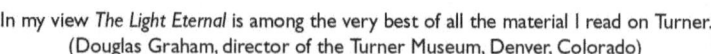
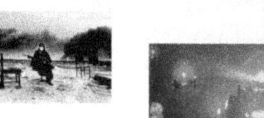

In my view *The Light Eternal* is among the very best of all the material I read on Turner.
(Douglas Graham, director of the Turner Museum, Denver, Colorado)

The Light Eternal is a model monograph, an exemplary job. The subject matter of the book beautifully organised and dead on beam. (Lawrence Durrell)

It is amazing for me to see my work treated with such passion and respect. (Andrea Dworkin)

Sex-Magic-Poetry-Cornwall is a very rich essay... It is like a brightly-lighted box. (Peter Redgrove)

CRESCENT MOON PUBLISHING P.O. Box 393, Maidstone, Kent, ME14 5XU, England
0044-1622-729593 cresmopub@yahoo.co.uk www.crescentmoon.org.uk